HISTORIC
AIRCRAFT
WRECKS

OF

SAN BERNARDINO
COUNTY

G. PAT MACHA

THE
History
PRESS

Published by The History Press
Charleston, SC 29403
www.historypress.net

Front cover: Lockheed Model 12 that crashed on Teifort Mountain on December 16, 1961, killing two men on board. *Courtesy Bob Koch. Back cover, left:* Tail assembly of Piper PA-31 that crashed in snowstorm near Big Bear Lake on February 16, 1992, killing seven people on board. *Courtesy George Petterson.*

First published 2013

ISBN 978-1-5402-2150-6

Library of Congress CIP data applied for.

To those who lost their lives while in military service on behalf of our nation and those who were aerial first responders lost on search-and-rescue, firefighting and law enforcement missions in San Bernardino County, California.

CONTENTS

FOREWORD

I first met Pat Macha in the fall of 2007 while researching a certain airplane crash in central California. His name popped up on a Google search when I typed in the words "aircraft wreck expert."

Boy, what an understatement!

I found out he lived just up the coast from me, so I cold-called him and told him about my project. He invited me to his home to discuss research. When I entered his garage, the spirit of the place overcame me. It was walled with file cabinets, maps and black binders representing literally thousands of detailed files, including one he "happened to have" on the topic of my research. Indeed, Macha's data is so organized and expansive, flight museums have vied for him to will the data to them in the event of his death. Macha—who is sometimes called an aircraft archaeologist due to his uncanny ability to piece together the history of a long-forgotten or rediscovered crash site from just a few seemingly insignificant pieces of wreckage—will tell you he's just a retired high school history teacher who has a lifelong fascination with aviation; but in the seven years he's guided me to various crash sites in California, I've come to describe him as the Indiana Jones of wreck hunters.

He's also a dedicated husband, father and grandfather who is emotionally attached to every story you'll read in this book. He has traveled to every piece of aircraft aluminum he mentions to deliver to you this historical treasure-trove of information. Pat has masterfully outlined the important role San Bernardino County had in aerospace history by weaving together the historical context of both the civilian and military aviation accidents that have occurred there.

Pat's first order of business whenever he visits a military crash site is to place a small American flag in the ground—a gesture of respect to those who lost their lives in the service of our country. I've stood beside Pat while he described to me with amazing detail why a certain plane went down, and almost every time he has done so, his eyes have welled up with tears. He often has photographs of the pilots, crew or passengers, which he logs in order to keep on hand in case a relative of one of the deceased ever wants to visit the location where a loved one lost his or her life. Pat and a tightknit group of fellow wreck hunters provide this service whenever requested. They call themselves Project Remembrance, and having been to a crash site at which Pat guided the son of a pilot who had been killed decades earlier to his father's final resting place, I can attest it was an emotionally charged moment of peace and closure when Pat guided him to what remained of the cockpit.

Through these compelling human-interest stories, Pat has raised my awareness of the historic importance of veteran and vintage crash sites and the need to respect and preserve them in not only this county's but also our country's rugged wilderness areas.

Because of Pat, I will never drive down a highway and look at the passing scenery—the mountains or deserts or just a brush-swept hillside—the same way. These places hold the remains of aviation history, and without people like Pat, we'd just keep on driving and never pause to reflect or pay our respects.

Eric Blehm
New York Times bestselling author of *Fearless, The Last Season* and *The Only Thing Worth Dying For*

ACKNOWLEDGEMENTS

This book would not have been possible without the help and encouragement of many individuals and organizations. They will be listed in chronological order starting from when I began researching and looking for aircraft wrecks in San Bernardino County.

1963–73: Fred Beam, Civil Aeronautics Board accident investigator; Inspector Willard Farquhar (RIP), San Bernardino Sheriffs' Department; Lennox High School Lancers Bill Finkbeiner (RIP), Dan Rico and Dave Herbert; Jerry and Jeffery Boal, United States Forest Rangers at the Barton Flats and Big Bear Lake Stations; James C. Risner (RIP), Camp Conrad director.

1974–84: Robert "Bob" Koch (RIP), retired USAF; Gary Salazar family; Major C.L. Burrell and Wyn Selwin, civil air patrol; Jon K. Lawson, David Chichester and Harry Krig; Captain Paul Stebelton, retired USAF and FAA.

1985–95: Bob Bhrule, civil air patrol; Rich Allison; Francis S. Yarnell; the X-Hunters Peter Merlin and Tony Moore; Jim Rowan; Joel Bishop; Ben Giebeler (RIP); John Zimmerman; Bob Lank; Robert Gates; and Elgin F. "Butch" Gates, San Bernardino County sheriffs' deputy, who knew the eastern Mojave Desert better than anyone I've ever met. He was enthralled by the Mojave's history and its beauty, too. He shared stories about old plane wrecks he found, and those he was still looking for. Butch passed away on December 30, 2009, and he is sorely missed by all who knew him.

1996–2013: Don Jordan; John Walker; Tom Gossett (RIP); Bill Gossett; David Van Norman and John Croaker, San Bernardino sheriffs, coroner division; Captain Alan Dow, civil air patrol; Nick Veronico; Trey Brandt;

Chris Killian; Jack "Suitcase" Simpson; Marc McDonald; Lewis Shorb; noted author Eric Blehm; Todd Loiselle; Jeff Corder; Chris LeFave; Ryan Gilmore; Thomas Maloney; David Mihalik; Dennis Richardson; David Lane; Bruce Guberman; Rick Baldridge; Mike Lyons; Jana Churchwell; Tony Accurso and his daughter, Evelyn; Walt Witherspoon; Fred Moore; Tim Baggerly of the Mohave Historical Society; Dave Trimble; Ingrid P. Wicken; Les Salm; Dan Catalano; Craig Fuller, founder of AAIR and provider of countless accident reports and photos; George Petterson, retired National Transportation Safety Board investigator, master pilot and aviation safety educator, without whose help the TB-25N, Bristol Mountains A-4C and Rim of the World Cessna 172 would never have been photographed or visited. Special thanks go to the American Aviation Historical Society for supplying many of the historic photos and to AAHS director Paul Butler for his help. Thanks also are sent to Jerry Roberts, commissioning editor for The History Press, and Ron Funk, webmaster for www.aircraftwrecks.com, who is responsible for scanning and resizing all images used in this book.

Finally, I thank my family for encouraging and supporting my avocation and for joining me in fifty years of hiking, searching and, sometimes, risking life and limb. I salute my parents, Charles F. and Mary Francis Macha (RIP). My father served in the Thirteenth Airborne Division, Eighty-eighth Glider Infantry Regiment during World War II, and his aerospace career spanned thirty-seven years. From him, I learned about aircraft structure and prefix numbers, not to mention a love of everything aviation related. My younger brother, Chris, and my sister, Cindy, started hiking with me in the 1960s. Mary Jane, my wife of forty-six years, has been on the trail with me since we started dating in 1966. Our son, Patric Joseph, and daughter, Heather Maureen, along with their respective families, have all participated in visiting crash sites in San Bernardino County and beyond. Our favorite place to camp in the San Bernardino Mountains is at Heart Bar Campground, just off Highway 38, near the old Star Route of times gone by.

INTRODUCTION

The year 2013 marks my fiftieth of searching for and documenting aircraft crash sites in remote locations throughout the state of California. I came to this unique avocation while working at a youth camp in the San Bernardino Mountains of Southern California in the summer of 1963. My camp job was hike master, which included nature walks, day hikes and overnight camping trips into the San Gorgonio wilderness. A highlight of the overnight trips included the ascent of Mount San Gorgonio, the highest peak in Southern California at 11,503 feet above sea level. The prescribed route to the summit was via the Poop Out Hill Trail Head to a bivouac site at Dollar Lake. After a night's rest, we hiked to the summit of "Old Greyback," where the view on a good day could be one hundred miles or more. Following lunch at the top, we reversed our course, picking up our packs and gear at Dollar Lake to begin the trek back to the parking lot at Poop Out Hill, where a stake-bed truck would return us to YMCA Camp Conrad in Barton Flats. We averaged eighteen and a half miles in two days on these wilderness treks. Continuous route repetition led me to try another way down from the summit where no trail existed in those years. On our first descent on the east flank of Greyback, we stumbled on the crash site of an air force transport plane that I recognized to be a Douglas C-47. Our group was dumbstruck as we surveyed a scene of devastation where wings, landing gears and engines were interspersed with personal effects, uniforms, shoes, luggage bags and headphone sets. Campers and counselors asked me what happened, when it had happened and who was on board. I wanted to know the answers to these questions, too. The aluminum structure looked new, bright and shiny. Our star-and-bar national insignia was visible on one of the wings and USAF on the other. I photographed the crash site that day with an Argus C3, 35mm camera borrowed from my father, from whom my love of everything airplane comes. I finally did learn the story of the C-47 tragedy from a U.S. Forest Service Ranger at Barton Flats Station who also shared with me the locations and stories of eight other aircraft crash sites that he had seen during his long tenure in the San Bernardino Mountains. This ranger had opened a door to the past, and I began the long search, which has continued to this day, for crash sites that are scattered across the mountains and deserts of California. Unlike roadside vehicle accidents that are quickly cleaned up and forgotten, aircraft wreck sites in remote locations remain largely undisturbed in deep canyons, hidden in forests, overgrown in the chaparral or widely scattered in small parts across vacant desert landscapes where few people venture.

San Bernardino County is 20,105 square miles of vast, mostly uninhabited lands characterized by seventy-two named mountain ranges, twelve named hills, eighteen major dry lakes and playas, with most of the aforementioned within or bordering the Great Mojave Desert. Other geographic features of note include Mountain and Cajon Passes, the San Andreas Fault Zone, Pisgah Crater and lava flow, Mitchell and Winding Stair Caverns and the Mojave, Santa Ana and Colorado Rivers.

The population of San Bernardino County surpassed 2.5 million in 2010. Five Interstate Highways transverse the county, including portions of historic Route 66 and State Route 395, which, along with dozens of county roads, provide access to many scenic mountain and desert areas. The federal government is the majority county landowner, with holdings that include military test, training and logistics bases as well as Joshua Tree National Park, Mojave National Preserve, San Bernardino National Forest and other open-space lands administered by the Bureau of Land Management (BLM). There are also two California State Parks, the Providence Mountains State Recreation Area and Chino Hills State Park.

Across this formidable area of mountain and desert lands are more than 425 aircraft crash sites where part or all of the wreckage remains to this day. These accidents often occurred in darkness and bad weather during military training missions, test flights and other "routine" assignments. Mechanical failures and a host of other factors were involved in these civilian and military losses. This book will offer the reader a glimpse into aviation accident stories, histories and mysteries in San Bernardino County, the largest California county and the largest in the nation, where I began my research and crash site documentation so long ago.

G. Pat Macha
Mission Viejo, CA.
2013

CHAPTER ONE

FLYING INTO THE STORM

From the earliest days of aviation in San Bernardino County, there were aircraft-related mishaps and major accidents. One such incident occurred on August 24, 1929, when a Lockheed Vega R393H was struck by lightning while flying in a thunderstorm east of State Highway 395 and north of Kramer Junction. Virgil Cline was an experienced pilot from Modesto, California, and the sole occupant of the speedy Lockheed monoplane when he crashed to his death as his Vega exploded in flight over the rugged slopes of Fremont Peak. Oliver Phillips, the superintendent of the Monolith Rand Mine, witnessed the Vega falling out of the clouds following a loud explosion. He was first on the crash scene and the first to know that Virgil Cline was dead. Rumors that the Pratt & Whitney nine-cylinder Wasp radial engine and other parts of R393H remained at the crash site led some wreck hunters to search the crash area without success in the fall of 1998 and winter of 1999. Finding any trace of Virgil Cline's aircraft would be considered an important discovery in the annals of aviation accident history.

Pilots were just beginning to understand that flying into thunderstorms or any mass of clouds could be dangerous. Nonetheless, on September 9, 1929, another Lockheed Vega, C859E, was lost while participating in the Los Angeles to Cleveland air race. On board was the veteran pilot Major John T. Wood, along with Ward Miller, his mechanic. Both men were wearing parachutes as Major Wood attempted to fly at night through a line of towering cumulus clouds. Ward Miller described flying in the severe turbulence when a wing suddenly came off and he was thrown clear of the disintegrating

The Lockheed Vega, a revolutionary design that modernized air travel in the late 1920s. *Photo courtesy AAHS.*

Vega. Miller pulled his ripcord and blacked out as he descended onto a flat area of the Great Mojave Desert about thirty-eight miles northwest of Needles, California. The next morning, the storm had passed, and the sun was shining when Miller started walking in the blistering heat of late summer. Ward Miller was lucky to find a cabin near Piute Springs as he trekked south. Though it was unoccupied, he found water there that helped save his life. After resting for a time, Miller started walking on the Searchlight Road toward Needles, and thirty-six hours after his bailout, he was finally rescued by a passing motorist. Ward Miller told the San Bernardino County Sheriffs in Needles that he doubted that Major Wood had been able to use his parachute. Sadly, that proved to be true when the pilot's body was finally located in the trackless Piute Valley near the widely scattered wreckage of his Vega monoplane.

The Lockheed Vega was a fine aircraft that set many records in speed, distance and altitude. Wiley Post, Amelia Earhart, Art Goebel, Ruth Nichols, Leland Schoenhair and a host of other aviation notables flew the famed Vega into the history books. The loss of Virgil Cline and Major John T. Wood, though tragic, helped other airmen and women avoid flying through thunderstorms that can occur in any season of the year.

Pilots in these early years often followed roads while en route from one landing field to another. Pilots still do it today, reinforcing the old joke that when a pilot filed an instrument flight plan with IFR, he meant "I follow roads." IFR actually means instrument flight rules, which are to be implemented when flying in darkness, clouds or storms. Most pilots flying in the 1920s and 1930s filed VFR flight plans, meaning visual flight rules. Visual flight rules are fine if the weather is good and the sun shining, but sometimes, pilots try to sneak through in marginal conditions by flying close to the ground under the clouds, commonly called "scud running." Scud running has been, and still is, a factor in many private aircrafts' weather-related accidents today.

On May 21, 1929, army air corps aviation cadet Henry W. Brummel was on a solo training mission from March Field in Riverside County. Cadet Brummel was following Highway 66 about fifty feet above the ground when he struck power lines draped across the roadway, causing him to crash one hundred yards from the pavement. It was a miracle that the young cadet was able to extricate himself from the cockpit seconds before his DeHavilland DH-4M AC-32932 burst into flames. Other pilots in a similar situation along the Cajon Pass/Route 66 flight path have not been so lucky.

With the advent of the first airlines came a new and revolutionary way to travel. Western Air Express was one such pioneer air carrier establishing service routes from Salt Lake City, Utah, to Grand Central Air Terminal in Glendale, California. A hallmark of any new air carrier was being able to field the latest air transport designs available. To this end, Western Air Express had purchased the Fokker F-10A trimotor airliner. On February 23, 1930, pilot James E. "Jimmy" Doles, copilot A.W. Bieber and flight steward John W. Slaton were returning F-10A NC-279E to Grand Central Air Terminal after dropping off their passengers in Kingman, Arizona. When NC-279E failed to arrive as scheduled, an air and ground search was initiated. Days passed without result until Dudley Steele, flying a Richfield Oil Company aircraft with Mrs. Juanita E. Burns as observer, spotted the smashed wreckage of the F-10A on rugged Shay Mountain located about eight air miles from Lake Arrowhead on February 29, six days after the crash. Jimmy Doles had encountered a winter snowstorm over the San Bernardino Mountains and crashed while flying blind apparently in an effort to stay on schedule rather than turn back and land at the Western Air Express auxiliary airfield, located near the top of Cajon Pass.

Sixty-three years would pass before Los Angeles–area resident and avid deer hunter Harvey "Harv" LeBlanc would stumble on the remains of the Western Air Express Fokker F-10A NC-279E on Shay Mountain. Mr. LeBlanc wanted to know what he had found, and he recovered parts from the once-proud airliner as evidence of his discovery. Mr. LeBlanc contacted me in the fall of 1993, and I was able to provide him with the history of this sad loss. My son,

Pat J. Macha, hiked to the F-10A wreck with his fiancée in 1994 to photo document what remained at the crash site, and what he found was a tangled mass of twisted, rusted heavy metal. The construction of the Fokker F-10A included a wielded metal structure, to which wood ribs were attached to create the airfoil shape. Doped linen and thin sheet wood was then applied to cover the structure, creating a wood-and-fabric skin. Several wildfires have burned over the crash site since 1929, destroying all the fabric covering.

The famed Notre Dame football coach Knute Rockne and seven others were killed on March 31, 1931, in the crash of a Fokker F-10A NC-999 near Bazaar, Kansas, when TWA Flight 591 flew into rough weather and a wing separated due to a combination of delamination and storm-related stress placed on the structure. The Fokker F-10 airliners were quickly replaced in airline service by the superlative all-metal Ford Tri-Motor and other new all-aluminum designs such as the Boeing 247 and Douglas DC-2. Nonetheless, the Fokker F-10 was a pioneer in the early days of air travel, with a few examples still surviving in museums today.

The Cajon Pass, which connects the Mojave Desert to the San Bernardino Valley to the south, has been the primary route for vehicle and rail traffic for more than a century and a half. With the dawn of aviation in the early 1900s, it became a fly route, too. When the Santa Ana winds were not blowing and clouds did not obscure the pass, it was a scenic pleasure to fly, but in darkness and poor weather, it became a plane catcher for the unwary, unlucky or inattentive pilot. In the 1930s, the army air corps lost five aircraft in or near the Cajon Pass.

One accident occurred on June 1, 1933, when USAAC Reserve second lieutenant Charles M. McHenry was flying a Fokker C-14A 31-388 transport aircraft from March Field in Riverside County to Crissy Field, San Francisco. The flight route included the Cajon Pass, western Mojave Desert, Tehachapi Mountains, Central Valley, Pleasanton Ridge and, finally, San Francisco Bay. This was an arduous flight for an experienced pilot, let alone a second lieutenant with just over three hundred flight hours and only three hours in the C-14A. Weather conditions were good except below and in the Cajon Pass, where stratus clouds were common at that time of year. Second Lieutenant McHenry followed the Santa Fe railroad tracks up the pass, flying under the clouds, to realize only too late that he was too low and too slow and that he was entering the clouds. The second lieutenant stated that once in the clouds, he "lost his sense of equilibrium" and that his engine "was losing power" also. Moments later, his left wing struck a mountainside, demolishing the fuselage and crushing most of the men inside.

Pat J. Macha at crash site of Western Air Express Fokker F-10A NC-279E. *Photo by Fred Moore.*

A USAAC Fokker C-14A similar to those that crashed in Cajon Pass in 1933 and 1937. *Photo USAAC Official via AAIR.*

Miraculously, Second Lieutenant McHenry sustained only minor injuries, while Sergeant Seymour R. Decker sustained serious injuries, along with Private Paul L. Blinka and Second Lieutenant Edward D. Kennedy, who, sadly, died in the hospital sixteen days later. Private Charles M. Ledbetter, Private Lawrence D. Romano and Private Addison C. Spencer were killed instantly in the crash. The Fokker C-14A had come down just below the top of Cajon Pass near Baldy Mesa. Army investigators determined that pilot error was the primary cause of the accident but that those who assigned such an inexperienced pilot for this mission were also to be held accountable. Although there was no post-impact fire, the C-14A was a total loss. The army board of inquiry was surprised that anyone survived this accident, given the circumstances.

Another Fokker C-14A, 31-385, crashed in Cajon Pass on May 5, 1937. USAAC captain Earl C. Robbins had departed Muroc Army Airfield at 3:45 p.m. Having just delivered needed supplies, he was en route back to his base at March Field. At 4:15 p.m., while flying at seven thousand feet over Cajon Station, the Wright 1750-3 engine stopped suddenly, and Captain Robbins immediately checked the fuel supply and flow to the engine. After switching fuel tanks and using the wobble pump, the engine still did not respond even though both tanks had fuel remaining. Captain Robbins looked for any open space where he could make an emergency landing, but seeing none, he elected to bailout, landing safely on a steep slope in the chaparral, where his only injury was a sprained ankle.

The C-14A glided on, finally crashing on a rugged mountainside. The army determined that the Wright 1750-3 had malfunctioned and that pilot error was not an issue. Captain Robbins noted that his aircraft had crashed almost intact and that he could see it from Highway 66 as he was being taken back to March Field. He was not the only one who could see the wrecked Fokker. Ben Giebler, a teenage aviation enthusiast, and his brother from nearby Redlands decided to hike up to the crash site with a friend. They did this within a week of the crash. Ben borrowed his dad's camera and snapped a few photos that have become key to documenting the history of this now long-forgotten accident.

Opposite, top: Wreckage of USAAC Fokker C-14A 31-385 that crashed in the Cajon Pass following bailout on May 5, 1937. *Photo courtesy AAHS.*

Opposite, bottom: Ben Giebler and his younger brother standing next to the cockpit of USAAC Fokker C-14A 31-385, circa 1937. *Photo courtesy Ben Giebler.*

Boeing P-12E USAAC pursuit plane, circa 1935. *Photo USAAF Official via AAHS.*

Near the bottom of Cajon Pass, the wreckage of USAAC Boeing P-12E 31-577 that disappeared on December 30, 1935. *Photo courtesy Ben Giebler.*

The Fokker C-14A was not the first crash site that Ben had visited. December 30, 1935, was marked by the disappearance of a USAAC Boeing P-12E 31-577, a biplane fighter flown by First Lieutenant John T. Helms. The young lieutenant was flying from Hamilton Field near San Rafael, California, direct to March Field when he disappeared in the vicinity of Cajon Pass. In mid-January, the USAAC posted a $500 reward for information leading to the location of the missing Boeing fighter and its pilot. The P-12E was finally spotted by chance on February 10, 1936, when two TWA pilots, Captain George Rico and First Officer Dana Boiler, spotted the wreckage as they flew their Sky Chief airliner by the southwestern flank of Cajon Pass en route to Grand Central Air Terminal. A ground search team arrived the next day to recover the body of Lieutenant Helms, but it was not found immediately. A mystery was in the making when the team found Lieutenant Helms's parachute in the cockpit of the P-12E and both the emergency food and water containers missing. Lieutenant Helms's body was finally located not far from his plane a day later. It appeared that he had survived the crash only to die of severe internal injuries as he attempted to hike down the mountainside.

Ben Giebler hiked to the P-12E site alone a few weeks after it was found. He was amazed that an airplane could remain undiscovered just a few miles from Highway 66 on the southeast side of San Sevaine Ridge that overlooks the mouth of Cajon Pass. Ben made several trips to the P-12E wreck, photographing it and recovering the vertical tail and rudder assembly. He kept his souvenirs until 1942, when he decided to help the war effort by bringing the aluminum P-12E parts to a reclamation center.

Ben Giebler went on to become a successful pilot and businessman in the Redlands area of San Bernardino County until he passed away in the 1990s. Ben's legacy comes from his interest in both aircraft wrecks and flying. Thanks to his photographs, we have a unique view of the early days of aviation in San Bernardino County.

When USAAC Reserve second lieutenant Robert C. Love and his passenger, Private Emory J. Parsons, departed from Grand Central Air Terminal in Glendale on March 27, 1937, for a seventy-mile night navigation training flight, he did not expect to have any problems. Second Lieutenant Love was flying the all-metal Northrop A-17 two-hundred-mile-per-hour attack aircraft. The serial number of his A-17 was 35-135. The number 35 indicates the contract year while the 135 indicates it was the 135th aircraft ordered by the army air corps in 1935. The A-17 was a stable, easy-to-fly aircraft equipped with the best instruments and radio and one of the finest engines of the time, a Pratt & Whitney 750-horsepower R-1535-11 radial.

Northrop A-17A, USAAC. Attack aircraft similar to the one lost on March 27, 1935, in the San Bernardino Mountains. *Photo courtesy AAHS.*

Second Lieutenant Love's flight plan would take him in a direct line to March Field in Riverside County with an anticipated flight time of forty-five minutes, but darkness and extensive cloud cover might have led the pilot off his intended course. Second Lieutenant Love tried to contact the March Field Radio Range to obtain navigational assistance, but the radio range had been offline since March 27. At 10:20 p.m., and again at 10:30 p.m., the A-17 was both seen and heard flying over the city of San Bernardino, with its navigational lights glimpsed, albeit briefly, through breaks in the clouds. Witnesses then heard the A-17 heading in a northeasterly direction away from the city lights and into the darkness over the San Bernardino Mountains.

When the A-17 failed to arrive at March Field as scheduled, a message was sent to all surrounding airports to alert them of the possibility that an army aircraft was in trouble and might need to make an emergency landing. At dawn on March 28, with no sign of the A-17 and its crew, a search was initiated, but clouds still obscured the mountains. However, word was received from the City Creek Conservation Camp that an aircraft had flown over its facility shortly after 10:30 p.m. on the preceding evening. The morning of the twenty-ninth saw the clouds dissipating, and army search planes from March Field began combing the San Bernardino Mountains in earnest. Shortly before 1:00 p.m., two forest ranges spotted the partially burned wreckage of USAAC A-17 35-135. The rangers summoned men from the City Creek CCC Camp to cut a trail into the crash site, where the badly burned bodies of Second Lieutenant Love and Private Parsons were recovered.

USAAC investigators reached the crash site on the following day and noted that the clock in the front cockpit of the A-17 had stopped at exactly 10:37 p.m. The plane's radio was dialed to the nonfunctioning March Field Radio Range frequency, 388 kilocycles. The pilot apparently had hoped that the radio range signal would lead him back to his base and out of the clouds and darkness that, unfortunately, claimed him. It was also determined that Second Lieutenant Love had flown straight up City Creek Canyon at full throttle until the plane collided with a pine tree, causing the left wing to separate from the fuselage, followed by the final impact that killed both the pilot and passenger instantly. The first wing of the general headquarters air force at March Field issued the following findings regarding the cause of the A-17 accident: Pilot error, 50 percent; weather, 25 percent; supervisory personnel, 15 percent; nonoperating radio beacon, 10 percent.

The burned and partly salvaged wreckage of the Northrop A-17 remains in the rugged poison oak–filled canyon recess where it crashed so long ago. Locals from the Fredalba and Running Springs communities have little idea or memory of the army fast-attack plane that disappeared on the night of March 27, 1937, while on a routine navigational training mission.

Many of the wrecks scattered across the deserts and mountains of San Bernardino County today are microsites, mostly removed for salvage or buried to make them less visible. One such historic aircraft wreck is a rare Consolidated P-30A, an all-metal, two-seat pursuit ship delivered to the U.S. Army Air Corps in 1935. Powered by a 700-horsepower Curtiss V-1570 in-line engine, the P-30A, later designated the PB-2A, had a maximum speed of 274 miles per hour, considered fast for its time. Only fifty of these two-seat fighters were built. Most pursuit planes had a one-man crew, but army planners were interested in providing the pilot with extra protection; hence, a gunner armed with a single .30-caliber machine gun was added, but not without the costs of increased weight and some loss of speed and range.

A flight of PB-2As assigned to the Twenty-seventh Pursuit Squadron was en route from Selfridge Field, Michigan, taking several days to reach Boulder City, Nevada, for its last overnight before continuing to Muroc Dry Lake in California to participate in the first large-scale war games to be held on the Mojave Desert. Muroc was to provide the army air corps with a temporary operating base where squadrons from all over the nation would congregate. The dry lake bed provided space for large numbers of aircraft. A tent city

The wing section of USAAC A-17 35-135 that crashed near the San Bernardino community of Fredalba on March 27, 1935, with fatal results for both crewmen. *Photo USAAC Official via AAIR.*

sprang up to house visiting airmen and their support crews. The desert skies provided space to practice dog fighting, bombing, strafing, mass takeoffs, landings and formation flying.

On May 27, 1937, the Twenty-seventh Pursuit Squadron was flying in formation toward its destination at Muroc when one of the pilots began doing chandelles west of Baker, some miles north of old Highway 91. While doing these maneuvers at very steep angles, the engine sputtered to a stop, and the PB-2A started to spin. The pilot, Aviation Cadet J.L. Schoch, immediately ordered his gunner, Corporal C.C. Sumner, to bail out, which he successfully did. Aviation Cadet Schoch stayed with the spinning plane trying every trick in the book to regain control, but without result. Finally, the pilot was forced to abandon his ship about one thousand feet above the desert. The PB-2A came down in a flat spin and was demolished on impact. Its pilot landed only one hundred yards away without injury, and the gunner arrived several minutes later, having bailed out at a much higher altitude.

Only moments before the crash, PB-2A 35-14 had been resplendent in the clear desert sky with its light blue fuselage and orange-yellow wings and tail. The U.S. Army Air Corps paint schemes of the 1930s were not designed for war but for high visibility, for all to see and know that when they looked skyward, it was an army plane that they saw.

It was just within the past decade that the first efforts were made to discover the location of this rare two-seat fighter of the 1930s. Noted researcher, pilot and wreck hunter Craig Fuller finally located the PB-2A crash site after several days of searching. What he found that confirmed it was the 1937 accident site were scraps of aluminum with the blue and bright yellow paint, still recognizable after seventy years of exposure on the Great Mojave Desert. I visited the PB-2A crash site in March 2013 to take a closer look at the accident scene. Interesting parts and pieces were everywhere, including the ubiquitous Lift the Dot cockpit interior snap found on almost every World War II–era U.S. military aircraft. Sections of yellow fabric that had once been attached to the rudder and elevators were found in a protected gully and still looked almost new. A cast-metal part with the Consolidated Aircraft Corporation prefix number 3021005 for the PB-2A was located, and many small parts were also found. Fire damage was noted on material associated with the nose section of the aircraft, but the flame had not spread and apparently burned itself out, preserving most of the fuselage, wings and tail. These sections were salvaged at a later date, presumably by the army or a metal salvager.

Aviation Cadet Schoch and his gunner were lucky to survive on that bright, clear and windless day in May 1937. The war games they missed went on as scheduled at Muroc, a harbinger of the real war that came just a few years later when the airplane and air power would become the decisive new weapons and arbiters of World War II.

CHAPTER TWO
THE WINGS OF WAR

Few people today know that in and around the Continental United States from 1941 to 1945, more than twenty-five thousand military airmen and women were killed in flight training, testing, ferrying, transporting or patrolling our skies and shorelines just prior to and during the Second World War. In California alone, there were 8,348 accidents involving the U.S. Army Air Corps and U.S. Army Air Force aircraft. No exact number of U.S. Navy, U.S. Marine or U.S. Coast Guard accidents are currently available, but they are estimated to be about half that of the U.S. Army. The U.S. Navy loss rates reflect the number of aircraft assigned to or passing through California. The lion's share of military aviation operations within California during World War II was conducted by the U.S. Army.

By 1940, Southern California was the fastest-growing center for aircraft manufacture in the United States. The weather was ideal for year-round flying, land suitable for airports and factories was available and railroad and port facilities made transporting raw materials efficiently easy. The population was growing rapidly as well, guaranteeing a viable workforce. Douglas, Lockheed, North American, Northrop and Vultee all became aviation giants during the Second World War. The Greater Los Angeles cities of Santa Monica, Long Beach, Inglewood, Hawthorne, Burbank and Downey became synonymous with aircraft construction. Consolidated and Ryan, based in San Diego, added to our aircraft production capability. Orders poured in initially from European countries facing invasion by the Axis powers of Italy and Germany. Orders also came from China, already at war with Japan. Thailand, Turkey and Brazil were buying U.S.-built warplanes, too. The U.S. Army Air Corps, U.S. Navy and the U.S. Marines were beginning to modernize their aviation elements with the latest fighters, bombers, transports, trainers and all manner of other aircraft types.

Our military needed new air bases for training, testing and housing first-line operational squadrons. San Bernardino County had the wide-open undeveloped spaces that were needed. The army already had Muroc Army Air Field in operation, used initially as a bombing and gunnery range. Though mostly located in Los Angeles County, the eastern part of the base is in San Bernardino County. Victorville Army Air Field near Highway 395 became the center for basic and advanced flight-training activities. Vultee BT-13 Valiants (BT stands for basic trainers), North American Aviation AT-6 Texans (advanced trainers), Curtiss AT-9 Jeep and Cessna AT-17 Bobcats were common sights in the skies around Victorville. Beechcraft AT-11 Kansan and AT-7 Navigator advanced aircrew trainers were joined at Victorville AAF by Bell P-39 Aircobras and Curtiss P-40 Warhawks used as advanced fighter trainers. The Consolidated B-24 Liberators arrived in 1944 to become "the operational bomber trainer" not just for pilots but also for bombardiers, navigators, radio operators and gunners.

El Mirage Dry Lake was an auxiliary airfield where Victorville AAF pilots could practice landings and takeoffs, sometimes in large formations. Gray Butte was another Victorville auxiliary located at the Los Angeles–San Bernardino County line. Hawes and Helendale were auxiliaries that are still used today for defense-related activities. During the early years of World War II, pilots received instruction in the Waco CG-4A troop carrying gliders at Victorville AAF. A host of other utility and transport aircraft were assigned to Victorville, including the Douglas C-47 Dakota and the Beechcraft C-45 Expeditor.

Twenty-nine Palms AAF, also known as Condor Field, was the center for glider pilots to train in small two-seat sailplanes, such as the Schweizer TG-3, Aeronca TG-5 and the Piper TG-8. Later in World War II, the navy and marines would establish air training and combat tactics bases at Twenty-nine Palms. Daggett Municipal Airport became a maintenance and modification facility for Douglas A-20 Havocs, and Chino Air Airport became a primary training field for army pilots operated under civilian auspices by Cal-Aero.

Another new army airfield was established east of the city of San Bernardino that was primarily a maintenance and repair facility. Once known as San Bernardino Army Air Field, it later became Norton Air Force Base (AFB), and today, it is a regional airport. The Ontario Army Airfield was home to numerous training units, including the Bell P-59A Airacomet jet fighter conversion unit. The critical need for pilots in 1941–43 led to the establishment of the civilian pilot training (CPT) program that helped relieve some of the pressure from military training bases. The CPT base at Silver Lake north of Baker was remote, with student pilots living in tents, in which they nearly froze in winter and baked in summer. The desert winds on the eastern Mojave Desert could be daunting, forcing fledgling pilots to stay on the ground for days at a time. When the winds were calm, however, the conditions were ideal for flying, with visibility unlimited. The easternmost AAF in San Bernardino County was located at Needles on the Colorado River. Around Needles were numerous auxiliary and emergency landing fields, some of which remain in use today.

In 1942, General George S. Patton came to the Mojave Desert to establish a series of training camps for desert warfare in preparation for the invasion of North Africa. These camps—Coxcomb, Essex, Goffs and Ibis—with their adjunct airfields became legends as General Patton created a mighty mechanized military power that integrated land and air forces into one of the most feared and respected armies in the world.

With the burgeoning growth of air traffic across San Bernardino County during the Second World War, there also came an aviation accident rate that few could have imagined. There were hundreds of incidents and major accidents that would claim the lives of more than 175 aviators, crewmen and passengers. One of the earliest losses was in 1940, before our entry into World War II, when North American Aviation delivery pilot Clyde L. "Bud" Hussey was killed while ferrying a factory-fresh Harvard Mk II advanced trainer for delivery to Canada. Harvard was the Royal Air Force name for the AT-6 Texan trainer flown by the USAAC. With Britain under attack, the Royal Air Force had moved most of its training bases to Canada or South Africa, as far as possible from the fighting raging in the skies over England.

The Harvard Mk II flown by Bud Hussey was painted in high-visibility yellow, a see-and-be-seen color that helped students avoid midair collisions and helped searchers to spot the plane if it were forced down or crashed. Hussey departed Mines Field in the Los Angeles area to fly to Palmdale, where he would spend the first night en route to his second stop at Las Vegas, Nevada. On January 19, 1940, Mr. Hussey was flying with three other Harvard Mk IIs in formation until clouds and fog were encountered east of Baker, California. All the pilots were briefed before takeoff to follow the highway to Las Vegas. Today, that roadway is the heavily traveled Interstate 15. Bud Hussey's colleagues noticed that he was not in formation after they

28

cleared Mountain Pass, with its snow-covered peaks, near Wheaton Springs, a small community astride the highway at Nipton Road. When Hussey failed to land at Las Vegas, he was posted as missing, and a search was launched.

Weeks passed, and intermittent poor weather hampered the aerial search effort. Ground searchers thought they would find the Harvard wrecked near the highway, and they hoped the bright yellow paint scheme would speed their discovery. Every military and civilian aircraft crew flying from or to Las Vegas was alerted to be on the lookout for the missing plane. On December 27, a report arrived in Las Vegas that two employees of the Morning Star Mine located seven miles south of Wheaton Springs on Highway 81 saw a low-wing yellow aircraft flying about one hundred feet above the Morning Star Mine Road, just below a dense cloud layer into which the plane almost immediately disappeared. On January 16, 1942, Pat Frank, a cowboy rounding up cattle for the Williams Ranch, found scattered parts of the Harvard Mk II, including a broken suitcase with Christmas cards signed by Bud Hussey. Mr. Frank reported his discovery to San Bernardino County sheriff Emmett L. Shay and then led the posse to the crash site, where the pilot's remains were recovered. The Harvard had crashed with great force and speed, ripping it asunder. The December 27 sighting of the Harvard was only five miles from where the wreckage was finally located. The authorities wondered what happened that caused Bud Hussey to crash here so far from his flight path. Some pilots thought Bud had lost sight of the main highway and had tried to turn around to fly back to Baker, where there was an airstrip. In doing so, he followed another road that led him into the cloud-obscured east flank of the rugged Ivanpah Mountains.

The story of the Harvard II does not end here. In the 1980s, Elgin F. "Butch" Gates began researching the story of the accident in which Bud Hussey lost his life. Butch had hoped to find an eyewitness who had gone to the wreck as member of the recovery team, but that did not pan out. His research did indicate that the site was east of Kessler Springs and north of the Ivanpah Cima Road. Unable to look for the crash site himself, Butch contacted me, and I, in turn, asked Lewis Shorb to follow up. Following two trips into the search area suggested by Butch Gates, Lewis "got lucky" and found the Harvard wreckage still wearing yellow paint after seventy years of exposure to desert sun, winter snow and dust storms. A few weeks later, I went to the Harvard site, situated in a rocky basin surrounded by Joshua trees, yucca plants and all manner of cactus. Looking down on the Ivanpah Valley, I wondered if Bud Hussey had ever seen the ridgeline that he was so fast approaching as he crashed on that stormy day in December 1940.

Above: Pat J. Macha holds the aileron with trim tab from North American Aviation Harvard MK II that vanished on January 19, 1940, while en route to Canada. *Photo by Chris LeFave.*

Left: Chris LeFave holds wing skin from the long-missing NAA Harvard MKII in the Ivanpah Mountains. *Photo by P.J. Macha.*

The saga of the Harvard Mk II would be the prologue for what was to follow in the dynamic and tumultuous days of World War II once the United States entered the fray on December 7, 1941. In fact, from January 1941 until the end of 1945, there were more than one thousand fatal accidents involving aircraft assigned to the army air force, navy, marines, coast guard, civil air patrol and the civilian pilot training program here in California. These losses, while not in combat, are sacrifices on behalf of our nation that should never be forgotten or diminished in any way. Fatal military aviation accidents in San Bernardino County totaled more than 140 during the war years, resulting in the loss of more than 175 lives. These losses were often eclipsed in the news media of the time by the gripping battlefield stories that electrified the entire nation.

The Japanese attack on Pearl Harbor had an immediate effect on military aircraft assignments and deployments on the West Coast of the United States. Coastal antisubmarine patrols and long-range reconnaissance flights seeking possible Japanese surface movements were initiated. Combat-ready fighter and bomber squadrons were flown to bases throughout California before being flown or shipped to the Hawaiian Islands to bolster defenses there and to other far-flung Pacific war fronts.

One such rapid deployment to the West Coast involved the Twenty-second Bombardment Group that included the Thirty-third Bomb Squadron equipped with brand-new Martin B-26 Marauder bombers. The B-26 was the fastest operational medium bomber in the USAAF inventory. Powered by two Pratt & Whitney R-2800 Double Wasp engines, the B-26 could achieve a top speed of 315 miles per hour. The bomb load was an impressive 4,800 pounds, and defensive armament included three .50-calliber and two .30-caliber machine guns. The normal crew complement was seven, including a pilot, copilot, bombardier, radio operator and three gunners. The early production series B-26s required highly experienced pilots because of high-wing loading, high landing speeds and other challenging flight characteristics.

Nicknames abounded for the B-26: "flying cigar," "widow maker," "flying coffin" and other epithets that will not appear in print here. Later versions of the B-26 resolved most of the aerodynamic problems, and the Marauder ended World War II with the lowest combat-loss rate of any medium or heavy bomber in USAAF service.

The Thirty-third Bomb Squadron deployed from Langley Field, Virginia, to March Field, California, on December 9, 1941. March would serve as home base, but most of the operational training time would be spent at

Martin B-26 Marauder
similar to 40-1475 that
crashed on Keller Peak on
December 30, 1941. *Photo
courtesy G.P. Macha Collection.*

Muroc Army Air Field on the high desert. Muroc afforded aircrews the opportunity to practice aerial gunnery, bombing and formation flying prior to their departure for Australia, where the B-26s would attack Japanese targets in New Guinea and elsewhere in the southwest Pacific theater of Operations. Before the Thirty-third could depart Southern California in February 1942, tragedy struck the squadron. About 4:20 p.m. on December 30, nine Martin B-26 bombers departed Muroc Army Air Field for a flight to March Field some seventy miles to the southeast. During the accident investigation, the flight leader, First Lieutenant Hubert J. Konopacki, stated that his flight was at 8,500 feet when it encountered "severe turbulence and heavy cloud cover over the San Bernardino Mountains, forcing all pilots to proceed on instruments." The updrafts over the mountains caused some B-26s to pop out above the clouds and others to plunge back into the clouds, dangerously close to the peaks below. It was not until First Lieutenant Konopacki landed at March Field that he realized one B-26 was missing. That aircraft was 40-1475, flown by Second Lieutenant Frank A. Kobal and his crew of nine on board.

An air and ground search was initiated on December 31, with Cajon Pass designated as the area in which the B-26 was most likely to be located. Gradually, the search area was expanded to include the eastern San Gabriel Mountains and the San Bernardino Mountains between Cajon Pass and Mount San Gorgonio. During the first two weeks in January, the search effort was hampered by periods of rain and snow. Finally, an army search plane spotted the wrecked Martin bomber on the highest mountain between Cajon Pass and Big Bear Lake: Keller Peak (7,887 feet). If the B-26 had been at 8,000 feet or had it been 300 yards east or west of its final course, Second Lieutenant Kobal and his crew would never have known what they had just missed, but tragically, their ultimate fate was not an option. The only solace we can offer the grieving next of kin is that they died instantly and did not suffer.

I first visited the crash site of the Martin B-26 serial number 40-1475 in the summer of 1978. By then, Keller Peak was the home for a USFS fire lookout tower. I parked on the dirt road below the tower and hiked into the buck brush and manzanita on the north side of Keller Peak, where I found landing gear legs, struts and a myriad of small parts and fragments. The most striking remnants were the two twin-row 1,850-horsepower Pratt & Whitney R-2800-5 engines, long-silent memorials for the nine USAAF crewmen who lost their lives in good service to our nation. One engine sits near the top of the ridge, and the other more than 150 yards below, resting next to a pine tree that is now a sentinel marker. My last visit to the site was in 2012. I climbed the steep stairs to visit the volunteer manning the Keller Peak lookout and to see the display of B-26 parts and a binder containing the accident history with photos of the crew and newspaper articles related to the B-26 loss. One striking piece of artwork on display is the commemorative painting by R.T. Foster titled *The Spirits of Keller Peak*, which depicts the in-flight B-26 approaching Keller Peak with the bomber's crew standing shoulder to shoulder in the background. On a clear day, the tower visit can provide a panoramic view of the San Bernardino Mountains, the crash site and how heartbreakingly close the B-26 came to clearing the peak itself. I then went on to visit the crash site, but the dense chaparral, legions of black ants and the possibility of stepping on a concealed rattlesnake limited what I could see of the remaining wreckage.

Today, a memorial plaque honoring the memory, service and sacrifice of the crewmen of Martin B-26 40-1475 has been placed near the crash site, thanks to the efforts of David G. Schmidt and Boy Scouts William and David Blake. David G. Schmidt's mother, Marie S. Schmidt, also played a key role

Memorial plaque on Keller Peak honoring the crew of USAAF Martin B-26 40-1475 for its service and sacrifice on behalf of our nation. *Photo by G.P. Macha.*

Opposite, top: The smashed wreckage of USAAF Martin B-26 40-1475 on Keller Peak west of Big Bear Lake. *Photo courtesy of former Lake Arrowhead fire chief Les Salm.*

Opposite, bottom: Close-up of tail gun position on the Martin B-26 in which nine USAAF aircrew died while en route from Muroc AAF to March AAF on December 30, 1941. *Photo courtesy of former Lake Arrowhead fire chief Les Salm.*

in researching the B-26 accident story and in helping to contact the surviving relatives of the B-26 crew. Once the USFS approved the placement of the plaque, a memorial gathering was arranged for August 12, 1995. David G. Schmidt and brothers William and David Blake helped to plan and facilitate the memorial ceremony that was attended by seventy-five people, including five next of kin from the B-26 crew.

August 12, 1995, was a day of remembrance and reflection for all who attended the memorial ceremony. With the plaque now permanently attached to a large boulder near the B-26 wreckage, the site has become a monument to those who lost their lives in the opening month of our entry into the Second World War. The scars on the land and the scars on the hearts of the next of kin and loved ones have lessened with time, but they are never really forgotten. Memorial plaques and markers help to make sure they never are.

A surge of training aircraft accidents began in 1942 as the wartime demand for qualified pilots became a top priority for all the service branches. Military aircraft losses in San Bernardino County included nineteen major accidents in which twenty-six airmen died and five others were seriously injured. All the aircraft types were training planes except for one, a Consolidated B-24D Liberator heavy bomber that suffered a double engine failure during a night navigational training mission on December 29. Five crewmen parachuted to safety, and four others crashed to their deaths in the Cady Mountains northwest of the small community of Ludlow, located on present-day Interstate 40. Desert explorer Lewis Shorb has hiked more than one hundred miles in and around the Cady Mountains searching for the crash site of Liberator 41-1100, so far without success.

Night navigational training accounted for another accident that killed five USAAF aviators on April 9, 1942. The aircraft was a Beechcraft AT-7 Navigator whose crew included a pilot, copilot, navigator instructor and two student navigators. The flight had originated at Mather Field near Sacramento, California, and was to end in Tucson, Arizona. At 8:40 p.m., the AT-7 crashed as it attempted to land at the Bagdad Auxiliary Airfield located just south of Route 66. Observers in the tiny community of Bagdad heard an aircraft approaching and reported seeing the red and green wingtip lights spinning just before the AT-7 crashed onto the dark desert landscape. Since no landing was scheduled at Bagdad Auxiliary Airfield, the army board of inquiry could not determine the cause of accident other than possibly pilot disorientation during an emergency-landing attempt. Witnesses stated they heard the engines roar just before the crash. Both landing gear were in the down position and were instantly torn off the aircraft as the AT-7 cartwheeled more than 250 yards across the desert.

Bagdad is a ruin today—only a few foundations remain from the old gas station and café. The desert is darker than ever on a moonless night. There is no monument marker for the crew of USAAF Beechcraft AT-7 serial number 41-21052. The crash site is widely scattered over a quarter mile of desert with 98 percent of the wreckage removed, but uniform buttons, parachute wrappers, instrument parts and one crew member's watch, along with other personal effects, are still there.

The following are the men whose memory we honor for their service and loss on April 9, 1942: First Lieutenant Richard W. Ford (pilot), Second Lieutenant William W. Hovey (copilot), Second Lieutenant Byron F.

THE WINGS OF WAR

Vandenburg (navigator instructor), Aviation Cadet Robert A. Baker (student) Aviation Cadet Leonard H. Ballif (student).

In 1943, accidents involving operational first-line combat aircraft became more common, including such types as the Lockheed P-38 Lightning, Bell P-39 Aircobra and Curtiss P-40 Warhawk fighter aircraft. Douglas A-20 Havoc and North American Aviation A-36 attack planes were also lost, along with more Consolidated B-24 heavy bombers. The Waco CG-4A troop-carrying gliders assigned to Victorville AAB would add to the growing list of accidents. Altogether, there were thirty aircraft destroyed with forty-one fatalities, but only one serious injury.

The Waco CG-4A troop-carrying glider entered production in 1942 for the USAAF, and more than seven thousand were built before production ceased in 1945. The CG-4A was designed to carry fifteen combat troops, including the two soldier pilots. The glider was built of tubular metal and plywood, and it was fabric covered. The CG-4A weighed up to 7,500 pounds when fully loaded. The Wacos assigned to Victorville were for glider pilot and tow pilot instruction. There were a series of CG-4A–related mishaps and crashes, including one in which the glider did a series of loops that it was not designed for. Happily, both pilots were able to parachute from their out-of-control aircraft near El Mirage Dry Lake on February 19, 1943. As the two pilots were descending by parachute, the CG-4A continued to loop between them before crashing on the desert. Another Waco crew was not as lucky a few days earlier when its CG-4A collided with another Waco glider while being towed in formation. The crew attempted to bail out as the stricken ship went into a graveyard spiral. Only the pilot was able to reach the door and jump. His copilot, trapped by centrifugal force, crashed to his death north of El Mirage Dry Lake.

Two fatal B-24 accidents occurred in the San Gabriel Mountains of San Bernardino County during 1943. The first was on March 5, when B-24D 42-40242 crashed on the southwest side of the Cajon Pass near Lytle Creek, killing all five crewmen when their aircraft broke up in flight. Army investigators speculated that the pilots had exceeded the design limits of the aircraft while on a training flight, causing catastrophic structural failure. Wreckage was scattered over nearly two miles of Lower Lytle Creek Divide. The second Liberator loss occurred on October 29 during a celestial navigational training flight while returning from Palmdale AAF en route to March Field. B-24E 42-7092, with a crew of ten, struck the south slope of 8,859-foot Cucamonga Peak at the 5,000-foot level, killing all on board. The bodies of the crew were not recovered for three days due to the rugged terrain. A combination of clouds and darkness were cited as factors in this accident.

"Bombs Away" was an official publication of the Victorville Army Air Field Bombardier School. In the August 1943 edition, the following quotation appears in a two-page layout honoring the loss of four airmen, two of whom were just one week from graduation: "The pain of war hurts most when it strikes from among us, men we deeply admire." These admired men were bombardier instructor First Lieutenant Bernard Corman and his bombardier students: Cadet Walter C. Vardon and Cadet Marshall Waxman. Second Lieutenant Allan R. Peterson was the pilot of the ill-fated Beechcraft AT-11 Kansan 41-27429 on the afternoon of August 13, 1943. Second Lieutenant Peterson had just completed the final bombing mission at 3:30 p.m. when he crashed into a 2,465-foot hill near Hinkley, about thirty-five miles northeast of the Victorville Army Air Field. The AT-11 crew ranged in age from twenty to twenty-four. They died together, instantly, on a routine and final training mission. For every name there is a face, and it is an honor to remember them here in these pages. The instructor and his students were in their prime, doing their part to help defend the Republic.

A nonfatal loss occurred on December 19, 1943, when a USAAF Cessna UC-78 Bobcat 43-7813 ran out of fuel in bad weather at night, twenty miles south of Barstow over the rugged Stoddard Mountains. What had started as a routine radio navigation flight from Kingman, Arizona, to Santa Barbara, California, was rerouted to land at Palmdale AAF. The pilot, Second Lieutenant Thomas O. Carson, was unable to hold the radio signal that would take him to Palmdale, and he became lost in the clouds and darkness east of Victorville, over the mountains of the Mojave Desert. At about 9:00 p.m., Second Lieutenant Carson radioed Palmdale that he had ten minutes of fuel remaining, that he had ordered his two passengers to bail out, and that he would follow them immediately. All three men parachuted into the rough Stoddard Mountains and hunkered down as best they could for the long, cold night. The next morning, Second Lieutenant Carson walked into the outskirts of Barstow. Less than an hour later, USN lieutenant (junior grade) Floyd L. Kirkman was picked up by a miner and driven into Barstow, where he was reunited with his pilot. Neither man had sustained any injuries. Major Henry C. Coles was rescued by San Bernardino County Sheriffs' Deputies at an old mining shack where he had taken refuge. Major Coles sustained major injuries from landing in a rocky area about a half mile from where the UC-78 had crashed and burned.

The army accident board cited the pilot for poor judgment and poor piloting technique. But Second Lieutenant Carson had not lost control of his aircraft and there had been no lives lost, so he was ordered to take

A Beechcraft AT-11 Kansan bombardier trainer similar to 41-27429 that crashed near Hinkley on the Mojave Desert, killing the crew of four on August 13, 1943. *Photo courtesy AAHS.*

Left: Bombardier student Cadet Walter C. Vardon, shortly before his death in August 1943. *Photo USAAF Official via Mrs. Loretta Kreft.*

Right: Bombardier student Cadet Marshall Waxman, as seen shortly before his death in August 1943. *Photo USAAF Official via Mrs. Loretta Kreft.*

a refresher course in radio navigation. The loss of the UC-78 was not considered "consequential" to the war effort. The UC-78 was also known as the AT-17 and "Bamboo Bomber" because it was constructed mostly of nonstrategic materials that included a wood main spar and wood ribs in the wings and tail assembly. The exterior surfaces were covered mostly by fabric that was doped and stretched tightly over the fuselage, wings and tail assemblies. The UC-78 was powered by two 245-horsepower Jacobs R-755 engines that were equipped with wooden propellers. With the landing gear retracted, the Bobcat could cruise at 175 miles per hour and cover 750 miles in optimum conditions. The conditions were less than optimum for Second Lieutenant Carson on the night of December 19, 1943.

The losses of 1944 in San Bernardino County reflect the military build-up taking place to support the worldwide operations of the armed forces of the United States. During this year, sixty-five aircraft were destroyed, and seventy lives were lost along with three serious injuries.

On March 3, 1944, Consolidated B-24E 42-1726 departed Blythe Army Air Field (AAF) with a crew of four. Second Lieutenant Edgar E. Lane was the command pilot, Second Lieutenant Allen S. Hassen the copilot, Staff Sergeant Robert D. Kirk the flight engineer and Staff Sergeant William C. DeCou the radio operator. Second Lieutenant Lane and his crew were tasked with flying their B-24E to San Bernardino Army Airfield, where modifications were to be completed. San Bernardino AAF was used during WWII primarily as a modification and repair center. In the postwar period, the San Bernardino field would become Norton Air Force Base, well known as a military air transport service, or MATS, base. When the B-24E failed to arrive, a search effort was immediately launched. The flight plan filed by Second Lieutenant Lane was from the Blythe AAF direct to San Bernardino following Highway 99 across the desert to the San Gorgonio Pass. The search effort was concentrated in this pass that was cloud enshrouded on the day of the flight. Mount San Gorgonio was especially scrutinized as the most likely place for the Liberator to have crashed. Old plane wrecks scattered across the desert wastes were spotted, examined and dismissed. The search effort involved not just aircraft but also civilian ski patrols that were sent into the snow-covered high country of the San Bernardino Mountains. After two intensive weeks of ground and air searching, the army air force scaled back the efforts to a "routine level" for pilots transiting the area to keep their eyes peeled. Finally, on May 6, 1944, USAAF pilot Major Arthur Blum Jr., flying from Palmdale AAF to the San Bernardino AAF, spotted the reflection of metal in the forest east of Cajon Pass. Ground teams were dispatched, and the crash site was finally reached

Consolidated B-24 Liberators were common sights in the skies over San Bernardino County during World War II, with eleven crashing there from 1942 to 1945. *Photo courtesy AAHS.*

on May 9, 1944. The B-24E wreckage was burned, mangled and scattered on the north slope of the mountains in a remote ravine above the West Fork of the Mojave River. Once the remains of the crew were recovered, the wreckage was dynamited to make it less visible.

More than 150 flight hours and over 3,000 man hours of ground search time had been expended before the B-24E was found. The searchers knew there was a flight plan, which was a well-known and predictable route from Blythe to San Bernardino. The record indicated the B-24E had departed Blythe at 6:22 p.m. and was expected to arrive at San Bernardino by 7:30 p.m. But the weather in the San Gorgonio Pass was deteriorating, and Second Lieutenant Lane possibly decided to fly around the north side of the San Bernardino Mountains in an effort to skirt the high country. But in the clouds and darkness, the B-24E began to descend too soon, perhaps because the pilots believed they were already in the San Bernardino Valley and near their destination. Tragically, they crashed just northeast of Sugarpine Peak at 7:20 p.m. The accident time was confirmed by a wristwatch found at the crash scene on May 9.

As the years passed, the B-24E wreck was forgotten and not visited, except by the occasional deer hunter who accidentally stumbled on the site or a pilot flying low and slow overhead. A metal salvager came to the remains of 42-1726 with his caravan of donkeys and a portable smelter in the 1960s to reduce the wreck's aluminum into ingots that he sold to make a living. What the salvager had no use for were stainless steel, armor plate, cast parts, the Pratt & Whitney R-1830 engines, landing gear assemblies and the machine guns not recovered in 1944, as these items could not be smelted or recycled.

Another visitor that stumbled onto the B-24E crash site was a solo hiker going overland through the woods in 1999. He was shocked to see the debris field that lay before him, and he spent some time trying to figure out what type of aircraft it was and when it might have gone down. One thing he never expected to see was a bone he thought might be human. He wondered if this was a missing plane, undiscovered until his accidental arrival at the site. Wisely, the hiker called the San Bernardino County Sheriffs' Department, and they in turn dispatched a team of sheriffs' coroner investigators who were accompanied by National Transportation Safety Board Aircraft Accident Investigator George Petterson and a few other parties with an interest in visiting historic aircraft wrecks. It was a privilege for my son and I to be included in this endeavor, for which my assignment was to find proof that we were in fact at the crash site of the USAAF Consolidated B-24E serial number 42-1126.

The hike began early on the morning of July 10, 1999, through a mixed forest of California live oaks, sugar pines and assorted chaparral plants characteristic of this transition zone. Thankfully, we encountered very little poison oak, and we reached our goal in just under one mile of mostly off-trail hiking. Before us lay all the telltale signs of the salvager's work: disassembled propeller hubs, the stainless-steel top turret ring and other heavy cast fittings of little metal value. As we surveyed the crash site, we thought of the aircrew members who had perished here. After several minutes of reflection, we went to work, the coroners in search of other crew remains and my son and myself after the "dog tags" of the aircraft: the data plates, stamped prefix numbers and inspector stamps. In a few minutes, we had located all the aforementioned items. The most important was a data plate with the Consolidated Aircraft Company prefix for the B-24, 32W9337; date of manufacture, 12-29-42; and the location of manufacture, Ford Motor Company, Dearborn, Michigan. Other parts yielded prefixes, 32B and 32D, all followed by a series of numbers that describes the exact location of the part on the B-24 airframe. Ford Motor Company converted assembly lines for cars to assembly lines for the B-24 in Michigan, while Consolidated produced the B-24 in San Diego, California, and Forth Worth, Texas. North

Debris from B-24E 42-1126 near Sugarpine Mountain included landing gear, propeller hubs and oxygen tanks. *Photo by G.P. Macha.*

American Aviation and Douglas also built the B-24 under license during World War II. All together, a staggering 18,482 B-24s were manufactured.

After three hours' work, the San Bernardino Sheriff Coroners completed their examinations of the crash site finding no additional crew remains. As we packed up for the hike back to our vehicles, two of the coroner investigators, David Van Norman and John Croaker, mounted a metal plaque on a large log overlooking the crash site that read, "In Honor of Those Who Perished in the Line of Duty, They Gave Their Full Measure of Devotion," followed by the names of the crew: Second Lieutenant Edgar E. Lane, Lieutenant Allen S. Hassen, Sergeant Robert H. Kirk and Sergeant William C. DeCou. The entire team gathered to pause and remember the flight crew of B-24E 42-1126. Many more B-24s would fall from the skies over San Bernardino County before the war came to an end.

The army air force was not the only service branch to lose aircraft and lives in San Bernardino County during 1944. Two Vought F4U Corsairs assigned to a marine corps fighting squadron based at MCAS Mojave in Kern County, California, collided on March 28, 1944, with a fatal result for one pilot and minor injuries for the other. The circumstances for the accident were not unusual for air-to-air gunnery practice, in which one aircraft tows

Above: Long-silent Pratt & Whitney R-2800 that was wrenched off USMC Vought F4U-1 Bu No 02649 following a midair collision with an aerial tow target on March 28, 1944. *Photo by G.P. Macha.*

Left: Tail section of USMC Vought F4U-1 Bu No 02649 in the foothills of the Slate Range in northern San Bernardino County. *Photo by G.P. Macha.*

a target sleeve while the other fires at it with six .50-caliber machine guns. F4U-1A Bureau Number (Bu No) 56303, flown by First Lieutenant Robert Bauman, who was towing the target sleeve, and Second Lieutenant Henry N. Lawson, who was making a firing pass in F4U-1 Bu No 02649 when he collided with the target sleeve and tow cable. The tow cable wrapped around his propeller and wrenched the Pratt & Whitney R-2800 two-thousand-horsepower engine from his Corsair, causing immediate loss of control and an ensuing flat spin from which Second Lieutenant Lawson could not bail out. First Lieutenant Bauman's Corsair was also knocked out of control, but he managed to bail out in the nick of time, landing safely in the desert southeast of the mining town of Trona. First Lieutenant Bauman's F4U-1A crashed in the Slate Mountains, while Second Lieutenant Lawson's F4U-1 came down on the desert with the R-2800 engine about halfway between the two Corsair crash sites, where it rests to this day.

Several mystery losses also occurred during 1944, including one on July 2, 1944, when a B-24J serial number 42-50780 with a crew of nine departed Muroc AAF on a practice bombing mission. After completing that mission, the Liberator was returning to base when it came apart in flight because of structural failure or, more likely, an explosion during a fuel transfer training procedure. There were no eyewitnesses, and investigators could offer no other possible reasons for destruction of the aircraft and the loss of the entire crew. After this accident, the investigators recommended that B-24 crews refrain from smoking, especially during fuel transfer operations.

A memorial marker was placed on the desert at the main impact by the son of the B-24J's flight engineer, Corporal Ralph A. Nestor. The memorial marker honors the loss of the entire crew of 42-50780. I have visited this site on three occasions since 2002, and the memorial is always festooned with flags and other mementos saluting the men who died suddenly and tragically northeast of Edwards Flight Test Center. A base known in World War II as Muroc AAF was once the home of the ill-fated B-24J and its crew. We found parts from the Liberator scattered along a line more than 1.75 miles from main impact, all of which was associated with the empennage and tail assembly of 42-50780.

For every name, there is a face, and for every fatal loss, there is a grave. There are the loved ones who remember their family members and friends lost during what General Eisenhower called "the Great Crusade" against the Axis powers in World War II. Second Lieutenant Pat L. Montgomery of Eastsound, Washington, was eager to become a fighter pilot and join the fight. Pat was twenty-one when he was commissioned at Luke Field,

Arizona, on June 27, 1944, and on July 14, he was assigned to Victorville AAF for advanced fighter training in the Bell P-39 Airacobra. The P-39 was a relatively small aircraft powered by the 1,200-horsepower Allison V-1710 inline engine mounted behind the pilot. This engine arrangement coupled with a short wingspan and fuselage length led to a high accident rate among inexperienced pilots. There was a popular pilot's song about the Airacobra's tendency to spin that included the lyrics "Please don't assign me to a P-39/I don't want to die before my time/In a plane that will tumble and spin." As with any aircraft, the P-39 had to be flown within its design limits, or, as pilots would say, "by the numbers." The tricycle landing gear made the P-39 easy to land and take-off. The Airacobra was a good fighter-trainer because of its speed, which made for an easy transition to an operational combat squadron flying the Lockheed P-38 Lightning that shared the same landing gear configuration and Allison engine. The pilot could access the cockpit from either side through automobile-type doors that had roll-down windows. In case of emergency, the doors could be jettisoned for easy pilot egress, except when the P-39 was in a spin; in that case, centrifugal forces could pin the pilot in his seat. The spinning could be so intense that the pilot usually lost consciousness prior to his ground impact and instant death.

Second Lieutenant Montgomery had accumulated 255 hours total flight time, including ten hours and ten minutes in the P-39, when on September 6, 1944, he lost his life after attempting an Immelmann flight maneuver in which his P-39 was seen to stall and enter a spin at about twelve thousand feet by a USAAF pilot flying nearby. The army air force accident investigators determined that P-39 42-18290 had impacted the ground in a spin and exploded and burned about twenty miles southwest of Victorville AAB because the pilot had attempted a maneuver expressly forbidden in the P-39 aircraft. It was recommended that all pilots flying the P-39 fighter trainer at the Victorville field be reminded of the "dire consequences" of not following the flight protocols for the Bell P-39 fighter series.

On January 24, 2005, Walt Witherspoon and I searched for and located the wreck of TP-39N 42-18290 almost exactly where Walt had predicted it would be. Less than 1 percent of the Bell fighter remained, but to our surprise, the pilot's wristwatch, I.D. bracelet and one dog tag were still at the crash site. These items were recovered and returned to the pilot's brother in Washington State after sixty-one years on the Mojave Desert.

There were 38 Women Airforce Service Pilots killed in the line of duty during World War II in the United States. There were 25,000 female

The much maligned USAAF Bell P-39 Airacobra, whose wrecks lie scattered across the Great Mojave Desert. The Airacobra served effectively as an advance fighter-trainer from 1942 to 1945 for many USAAF pilots. *Photo courtesy AAHS.*

applicants for the Women Airforce Service Pilots, or WASP program, but less than 2,000 were accepted. Of those, only 1,102 graduated. The WASPs were all volunteers who wore uniforms and followed military regulations and protocols, but they were not in the military. If they were killed or injured, it was the responsibility of the WASP families to bury the dead and provide care for the sick or injured. WASPs were not allowed to marry, but some did secretly. One of those who did was Marie Michell, a very attractive twenty-year-old who was assigned to the Victorville Army Air Field in the fall of 1944. Marie was one of the few women who had learned to fly before joining the WASPs, which she graduated from in the Class of 44-W-2 at Avenger Field, Sweetwater, Texas, on March 11, 1944. After graduation, Marie was assigned to the Fifth Ferrying Group at Love Field in Dallas, Texas. The Fifth Ferrying Group was part of the Air Transport Command, and the Fifth was tasked with delivering factory-fresh army aircraft of all types to bases around the Continental United States for operational use or shipment overseas. Marie was secretly married to a U.S. Army flight surgeon, Major Hampton C. Robinson, two weeks before her fatal accident on October 2, 1944, while flying in a B-25D Mitchell bomber.

The pilot of the B-25D was First Lieutenant George Danilo Rosado from San Diego, California, a twenty-seven-year-old family man with two young sons. The third member of the flight crew was Staff Sergeant Gordon L. Walker, who was also a married father with a two-year-old son. While Staff

Sergeant Walker was listed as a passenger on the B-25D, it is believed he was acting as a crew chief for the training flight. One important mission of the crew chief was to manually lower the landing gear and flaps in case of hydraulic failure. Marie Michell Robinson was a substitute copilot for another WASP who was unable to report on the assigned day.

First Lieutenant Rosado had 1,521.5 flight hours prior to his transition training flight in B-25D 41-30114 on October 2, 1944, but only 4 of those hours were in the B-25 aircraft type. Lieutenant Rosado departed Victorville AAF at approximately 1:15 p.m. local time in clear weather. Second Lieutenant Lawrence A. Beishel, the pilot of a Bell P-39, reported that he observed a B-25 descending toward the desert floor in a spin. Lieutenant Bieshel also reported that no parachutes were observed and that he saw the B-25D crash and catch fire at 1:40 p.m. The time of the accident was later confirmed when Marie Michell Robinson's watch was found stopped at that time exactly.

The army safety board determined that the pilot had allowed the B-25D to stall and enter a spin from which there was insufficient altitude to recover. Who was actually flying the aircraft at the time of the accident could not be determined, but it was assumed that First Lieutenant Rosado was at the controls. Centrifugal forces would have trapped the crew within their spinning aircraft, making escape almost impossible. The flight manual for the B-25 aircraft states that pilots should not intentionally spin this aircraft under any circumstances. Flight voice recorders and black boxes did not exist in the World War II era, so we will never know what was being discussed by the youthful crew of 41-30114 as they flew on a westerly heading from Victorville Army Air Field and into history.

Marie Michell Robinson's body was accompanied by her husband to Troy, Michigan, for burial. Marie's family paid all the transportation and burial expenses. First Lieutenant Rosado was interred with full military honors at the Fort Rosecrans National Cemetery in San Diego, and Staff Sergeant Walker was buried at Stockton, California.

In 2005, I was contacted by Ronald D. Rosado, the son of First Lieutenant George D. Rosado, about the possibility of locating the crash site of his father's B-25D. Thanks to a lead from a friend, we were able to locate the crash site, confirming that it was a B-25D by the presence of many small parts with North American Aviation prefix numbers for the B-25 series of aircraft. What surprised our team was the discovery of personal effects that could be associated with each of the three crew members. A wrist identification bracelet, part of a charm bracelet, a WASP insignia, uniform wings and a gold ring all belonged to Marie Michell Robinson. Silver pilot's wings, a Bulova wristwatch, lieutenant's uniform bars and other personal effects belonged to First Lieutenant George D. Rosado. In 2005, all of the aforementioned items were returned to next of kin, thanks to efforts of the Project Remembrance Team. It was not until 2012 that Staff Sergeant Gordon L. Walker's next of kin contacted me, and arrangements were made for a site visitation and the return of a ring, keys, assorted coins and a comb belonging to Staff Sergeant Walker.

WASP Marie Michell Robinson was killed in the crash of a USAAF B-25D Mitchell bomber on October 2, 1944. She was twenty years old at the time of her death. *Photo courtesy World War II WASP Museum.*

On November 12, 2005, the Rosado family gathered at the crash site to place a memorial plaque honoring the memory, service and sacrifice of those who lost their lives aboard the USAAF B-25D Mitchell bomber on October 2, 1944. Tears flowed, and prayers were said as the plaque was set in concrete. Ron Rosado, the pilot's son, said, "Now we have closure—being here means so much to all of us." In January 2013, the grandson of Staff Sergeant Gordon L. Walker and his wife visited the crash site, where they, too, found a measure of peace and closure. Command Sergeant Major Gordon S. Walker wears his grandfather's name well as he continues his service on behalf of our nation as a proud member of the United States Army.

As 1944 drew to a close, the Allies were advancing on all fronts, and the production of certain training and combat aircraft was being scaled back, which included some planned reductions in pilot and crew training, too. The last fatal military aviation accident in San Bernardino County in 1944 took place on December 7, when a USAAF Lockheed P-38L Lightning 44-23806 crashed twelve miles south of Victorville AAF. The pilot, Flight

Officer Richard S. Secor, was part of a flight of four P-38s engaged in air-to-air combat tactics training when he apparently lost control of his P-38 and crashed to his death. The army board of investigation concluded that the pilot might have stalled his aircraft or that the life raft dingy carried on board for over-water flights might have inflated accidentally and caused the pilot to lose control.

A decline in military aircraft accidents in 1945 reflects the scaling back of pilot and crew training activities in San Bernardino County. Twenty-six aircraft were destroyed, and twenty-five airmen were killed while three sustained serious injuries. Most of the 1945 losses involved operational combat aircraft assigned to advanced training activities. On January 6, a USAAF Bell P-39Q 44-3504 crashed and burned twelve miles southwest of Victorville AAF, but the pilot managed to bail out, sustaining serious injuries. On January 9, a Lockheed P-38L 44-24337 was lost near Daggett during a forced landing on a dry lake bed, in which the pilot escaped his burning fighter, also with serious injuries.

The first fatal 1945 accident in the county took place on January 30. It involved a Ford Motor Company–built B-24L-FO 44-49180 that had departed Victorville AAF at 2:10 p.m. for a simulated radar-bombing training flight with a crew of six on board. The Liberator had the minimum flight crew for this mission, including First Lieutenant James G. Wright, pilot; Second Lieutenant Norbert J. Vehr, copilot; and Technical Sergeant Harvey L. Cook, flight engineer. The radar bombardier instructor was Second Lieutenant Carl F. Hansen, and his students were Second Lieutenant John R. Palin and Second Lieutenant Herbert A. Perry. Shortly after takeoff, Second Lieutenant Hansen smelled smoke in the area of the bomb bay and notified the pilot, who sent Technical Sergeant Harvey Cook to investigate. Almost immediately, the number-two Pratt & Whitney 1830 engine began to vibrate wildly, and the pilot tried to feather the propeller and shut the engine down, without success. At this point, First Lieutenant Wright ordered the crew to bail out, and Second Lieutenant Hansen, along with one of his students, Second Lieutenant Palin, departed the aircraft immediately. At this point, the B-24L was only about two thousand feet above the desert floor and starting to enter a left turn with fire visible behind the number-two engine. Moments later, 44-49180 crashed and burned in the desert about eighteen miles north of Victorville Army AAF.

Second Lieutenant Hansen told investigators that when he bailed out, Technical Sergeant Cook was standing on the catwalk in the bomb bay with his parachute on and that Second Lieutenant Perry was seated in the empennage of the plane with no parachute attached to his harness. Technical Sergeant Harvey Cook hesitated to bail out as he might have been trying to encourage Second Lieutenant Perry to attach his parachute and jump. Technical Sergeant Cook might also have thought the B-24L was too low for a successful bail out and that a crash landing on the desert was his best chance for survival. We will never know exactly what happened aboard 44-49180, but we do know what the highly experienced and combat-decorated technical sergeant told his newly married wife, Loretta. He said that morale was low at Victorville Army Air Field and that he was very worried about the poor-quality maintenance being done there. He also said that he felt safer in the India/China/Burma Combat Theater of Operations with the Tenth Air Force, where morale was high and the quality of maintenance work was excellent. Technical Sergeant Harvey L. Cook knew the B-24 Liberator well, having flown dozens of bombing missions as a turret gunner over Japanese-held Burma, Mandalay, Thailand and Andaman Islands in the Indian Ocean. Technical Sergeant Cook earned the Air Medal, Distinguished Flying Cross, Purple Heart and the Asiatic-Pacific Theater Ribbon. His death came as a terrible shock to his new wife, Loretta. They had been married for seven months, and during that time, they had only six weeks together before the accident. Loretta Cook was working at a defense plant in the Chicago area when she received a telephone call from her landlady that a telegram from the War Department had arrived. When Loretta returned home that evening, she was given the yellow envelope with the sad news that her young husband was dead, killed along with three others in the crash of a B-24 bomber. The army shipped the body of Technical Sergeant Harvey L. Cook to Illinois, promising fifty dollars to pay for his interment.

In 2002, a search effort was launched to locate the crash site of B-24L 44-49180. A group of interested individuals, including me, began combing the desert north of the old Victorville Army Air Field without success until Rick Baldridge, a highly skilled computer programmer from Northern California, brought new technology into play that helped compute the distance from a known terrain feature that guided us to a place on the desert within a few yards of the crash site. Even though less than 1 percent of the B-24L remained, we did find small parts with the prefix numbers that verified the wreckage was that of a Ford Motor Company–built Consolidated B-24. A survey of the site revealed a dog tag, a ring and other items belonging to Technical Sergeant Harvey L. Cook. With these items collected, another search was launched, this time to locate the next of kin of Staff Sergeant Cook and other members of the crew. A writer for the *Los Angeles Times*, Gil H. Reza, was able to locate next of kin for two of the deceased B-24Ls six crewmen and one survivor, Second Lieutenant Carl F. Hanson, who provided a gripping eyewitness account of his final minutes aboard the doomed Liberator. Another key find was that of Technical Sergeant Harvey L. Cook's beloved wife, Loretta, living in Woodstock, Illinois. Loretta had remarried to become Mrs. Loretta Kreft. She raised two children and was widowed for a second time in 2003. In a telephone interview with me in 2004, she expressed her gratitude for the return of her husband's personal effects but said, "sadness arrived with the package also." Loretta said, "Harvey Cook was her first true love" and that she had continued to wear a watch he had given her in 1944. "We were very happy together, but the fortunes of war changed all of that."

Midair collisions took their toll in 1945, starting with the loss of two USAAF P-38L fighters on February 12, high above the rugged Avawatz Mountains north of Baker, California. Captain William D. Horton, age twenty-six from San Diego, California, was apparently able to bail out of his stricken aircraft but was unable to open his parachute in time to save his life. Twenty-four-year-old Captain Donald L. Webber of Compton, California, was unable to bail out and rode his P-38L into the ground with a fatal result. I visited the crash sites of both P-38Ls in March 2007 on a cold and windy day with the stark terrain of the Avawatz Mountains providing a vivid backdrop to the widely scattered wreckage of the two fallen Lightnings. A large wood *X* marked the crash sites, but the yellow paint had faded completely, bleached bare by sixty-two years of sun and wind.

Technical Sergeant Harvey L. Cook shown here with his wife, Loretta, shortly before his death on January 30, 1945, in the crash of USAAF B-24L 44-49180. *Photo courtesy Loretta Kreft.*

The flag of remembrance and respect flies at the crash site of USAAF Lockheed P-38L 44-24790, whose pilot, Captain William D. Horton, was killed in a failed bailout attempt following a midair collision on February 12, 1945. *Photo by G.P. Macha.*

Two more USAAF Lockheed P-38Ls were lost when they collided and exploded ten thousand feet above the desert while making passes at a tow target. Wreckage was scattered over two square miles on Superior Dry Lake north of Barstow. Killed in the accident were twenty-four-year-old Second Lieutenant Walter Mogensen of Modesto, California, and Second Lieutenant Earl A. Morgan. It was thought that both pilots were killed instantly in the collision. Scattered remnants of shattered P-38Ls can still be seen on Superior Dry Lake and the surrounding desert, silent reminders of the World War II era in San Bernardino County.

The U.S. Navy suffered numerous losses in the county in 1945, including that of two dive bombers flying from the Naval Auxiliary Air Station at Twenty-nine Palms. The first occurred shortly after takeoff on April 16, killing twenty-six-year-old Lieutenant (junior grade) George Henry Allred of Birmingham, Alabama. The second accident on April 18 killed Lieutenant

Victor C. Ideuo during dive-bombing practice twenty miles northwest of the air station.

The loss of a navy or marine North American SNJ-4 in the San Bernardino Mountains is still something of a mystery insofar as the accident date. While working summers in my high school and college years at a YMCA camp in the Barton Flats area, I talked with several veteran U.S. Forest Service Rangers who told me stories of airplane crashes they were familiar with, and one of these occurred late in World War II on Moon Ridge south of Big Bear Lake. It was winter, and the area mountains were blanketed in snow and often obscured by clouds. Two young naval aviators were lost flying up the Santa Ana River canyon when suddenly a mountain ridge appeared through the cloudy mists. The pilot, realizing he could not clear the ridge, pancaked his training plane on the only small flat area along the entire ridgeline. The heavy packed snow cushioned the impact, and both pilot and passenger survived. The only serious injury was a broken arm suffered by the passenger. The pilot apparently knew that the community of Big Bear Lake was nearby, and he decided to hike there for help, leaving his passenger inside the aircraft, which had an enclosed cockpit, affording some protection from the elements.

After more than three hours of tough climbing and hiking, the pilot finally found help, and a rescue party was quickly formed. The injured passenger was safely removed from the wrecked plane and taken to the infirmary in Big Bear and, from there, to a hospital in San Bernardino. When the winter snows melted, navy accident investigators visited the crash site and determined that only the cockpit instruments and the two .30-caliber machine guns could be salvaged. Because the SNJ-4 was intact, the navy elected to dynamite the wreck to make it less visible. Years later, the SNJ was still being reported by pilots flying in the area, so the civil air patrol sent in a ground team to paint yellow Xs on the wings and engine, indicating this was a known wreck that need not be reported.

In the summer of 1964, I first visited the SNJ-4 crash site after descending from a ridgetop through a painfully dense growth of buckthorn that impaled my legs and forearms. The visitation was worth the trouble, though, with 80 percent of the SNJ-4 still recognizable, including the outer wings, fuselage, landing gear, empty .30-caliber ammunition boxes and the long-silent 550-horsepower Pratt & Whitney R-1340 radial engine. Here was a military crash site where, because of piloting and luck, two aviators had survived what in most similar cases would have been a fatal or very serious injury accident.

The port outer wing section of USN North American Aviation SNJ-4 Texan trainer, circa summer 1964. Two navy airmen survived this crash south of Big Bear Lake during or shortly after World War II. The accident date is still a mystery. *Photo by G.P. Macha.*

Charles F. Macha, my father, worked for North American Aviation most of his adult life, and he told me what to look for in making a positive identification of any crash site I might visit. Find the data plates attached to the wings, ailerons, flaps, land gear doors and internal tubular metal structure. These plates will identify the aircraft type and version and, sometimes, the date of construction. Prefix numbers followed by part numbers will indicate exactly what type of airplane wreck you're looking at and where exactly the parts are located on the aircraft. Inspectors' stamps and the manufacturer's symbols or logos will offer additional proof of what has been found. The SNJ-4 wreck had more data plates, stamps, prefix numbers and part numbers than one could shake a proverbial stick at. From that summer day in 1964 forward, I knew exactly what to look for, thanks to my dad.

A USFS ranger told me about another "old wreck" from World War II up in Fish Creek Meadow near the boundary with the San Gorgonio wilderness. Again, similar to the SNJ-4 story, but with army pilots on board, a forced landing had been made in a small meadow at about eight thousand feet mean sea level (MSL) with both pilots surviving. The airplane was intact and was left right where it had crashed. In the summer of 1964, during a day off from camp, I drove with a friend to Heart Bar Ranch, where beef cattle spent their summers feeding in the lush alpine meadows. It was here that we found the fuselage of a Boeing/Stearman PT-17 minus its engine, wheels and all the fabric covering. I was able to climb into the back seat of the old trainer and imagine what it might have felt like to crash-land in a remote and unfamiliar mountain area. Recently, Craig Fuller of AAIR was able to locate the accident report for this mishap, and I was finally able to learn more details.

On July 15, 1945, Second Lieutenant Willis J. Miller and Second Lieutenant Edward J. Modes were assigned to fly Boeing/Stearman PT-17 NC53475 from Heron Field near Blythe, California, to Riverside Municipal Airport, where the plane was to be taken out of service with the civilian pilot training program and sold at auction. The war was winding down, and the civilian pilot training program had been cancelled. The cause of the accident was officially listed as carburetor failure. Second Lieutenant Miller, the pilot, suffered chest contusions and a broken left arm, while Second Lieutenant Modes sustained superficial contusions and bruises to the face and neck. Both men hiked several miles down into the South Fork of the Santa Ana River, following it to where Highway 38 ended in those days. A young married couple was picnicking by the streamside when two army flyers walked up, asking for help. The couple provided the flyers with something to eat and then drove them to hospital in Redlands. In 1964, the camp where I was employed had a craft director that had been one of those who had helped the army pilots nineteen years earlier. She had forgotten the airmen's names but said that "they were nice boys who we were glad to help."

The last B-24 accident in San Bernardino County occurred on July 18, 1945. Following an engine fire, the pilot, Captain Walter P. Graham, rang the bailout bell. All six crewmen bailed out successfully with only the bombardier, Flight Officer William W. Sephton, being injured. He sustained

Two USAAF pilots survived a forced landing in a remote area of the San Bernardino Mountains on July 15, 1945. The Boeing/Stearman biplane trainer was abandoned on site, and its fabric covering deteriorated with time. I enjoy a fantasy flight from the back seat of the PT-17, circa summer 1964. *Photo by Al Delganante.*

minor burns and a broken ankle. The accident scenario, which started with a fire, was not uncommon, but the ending was unusual in that the burning B-24L 44-49562 crash-landed intact on a flat stretch of desert between the North and South Shadow Mountain Ranges west of Highway 395, as if the pilot made a forced landing. The fire burned itself out, leaving the outer wings and tail assembly in recognizable condition. Less than 1 percent of 44-49562 remains today.

Three additional fatal accidents brought 1945 to a close in San Bernardino County. A USN Vought F4U-1D Corsair Bu No 82818, flown by USNR ensign Elbert W. Weaver of Thayer, Missouri, was seen by witnesses flying east in clear weather when it collided with an 8,800-foot ridge near Forest Home in the San Bernardino Mountains on August 10. Two puffs of smoke were observed as the F4U-1D skipped along the ridgeline. An aerial search launched that same day could not spot the wreckage of the Corsair. Ensign Weaver was posted as missing, and no further search missions were flown. Finally, on September 17, two high school–age boys hiking up Mill

Creek came upon human remains and aircraft parts. They reported their discovery to USFS rangers, and San Bernardino County coroner R.E. Williams was called to investigate. Within a few days, the remains were confirmed as those of the missing ensign. It was then realized that a powerful thunderstorm in early September had washed both the remains of the pilot and the F4U-1D parts into the canyon bottom. Members of the Project Remembrance Team and I conducted a search for the Corsair wreckage in June 2007, and we were able to locate a landing gear assembly along with other small, assorted badly rusted parts. We were unable to locate any other wreckage after climbing high into the steep ravines near Little San Gorgonio Peak.

On August 10, a USAAF Lockheed P-38L 44-24492 crashed, killing Lieutenant Kenneth R. Frost thirty miles north of Daggett near Langford Lake, and finally, a USAAF Curtiss C-46A Commando 41-5190 transport crashed on October 2 en route from Ontario AAF to Reno AAF. The flight departed at 1:00 a.m. and was supposed to fly through Cajon Pass on Blue Airway 14, but for reasons known only to the pilot, the C-46A flew northwest, toward the towering 10,069-foot Mount San Antonio, the highest peak in the San Gabriel Mountain Range. Flying in darkness and clouds, the doomed army transport struck the south flank of Old Baldy about 300 feet below the crest and continued careening into the saddle between East and West Baldy before plunging over the north side, leaving a trail of debris and death behind. While the initial impact was in San Bernardino County, the majority of the wreckage was scattered into Los Angeles County, where it can be seen today from Highway 2 reflecting the sun's rays and shining like a diamond on the nearly vertical north flank of Mount San Antonio. An outer section of wing remains on the south slope of the mountain in an area of manzanita and pine trees within San Bernardino County. Killed in the crash were Major Ovid F. Pinckert, pilot; Second Lieutenant Edwin M. Mize, copilot; Corporal Barney Cummins, flight engineer; and Second Lieutenant Martha S. Betts, women's army corps nurse, the only passenger.

The Second World War ended, and one of the last military accidents of 1945 occurred on flat desert near Mountain Pass north of the present-day I-15 when Second Lieutenant Edwin C. Schultz made a precautionary gear-up landing due to a low-fuel state. Damage to the USAAF T-6C Texan trainer was substantial, but the pilot escaped without injury. One chapter in aviation history was ending, and another was about to begin as the dawn of the jet age brought great changes to the skies above San Bernardino County.

CHAPTER THREE
SKY'S THE LIMIT

The end of the Second World War heralded a new age in aviation for San Bernardino County. Not only was the United States of America the most powerful nation on earth militarily, but we were also the hands-down leaders in the world of technology. The Southern California aviation industry was on the cutting edge of new military jet designs and manufacturing, along with new airliner production to meet the pent-up demand for long-range, comfortable passenger aircraft. Just as postwar automobile production was ramping up, so too was the production of inexpensive and versatile light aircraft for use by the postwar public that included thousands of former service men and women who wanted to continue flying on a recreational or business basis.

On September 18, 1947, the United States Air Force was established as a separate branch of the armed services. San Bernardino Army Airfield became a USAF base, called Norton Air Force Base in 1950, and Victorville Army Air Field became George Air Force Base. Ontario Army Air Field became an Air National Guard (ANG) Base in joint use with civilian, airline and aircraft manufacturers Lockheed and Northrop. Small civilian airfields popped up all over San Bernardino County, reflecting the rapid growth of the general aviation sector. The Cold War and the Korean Conflict guaranteed that military bases in San Bernardino County would continue to be of vital importance to our national security.

George AFB on the high desert would become home to Tactical Air Command fighter-bombers, including the Republic F-84 Thunderjets, F-86

Sabers, F-100 Super Sabers and, later, the Lockheed F-104 Starfighters, Republic F-105 Thunderchiefs and McDonnell F-4 Phantoms. Norton AFB became a Material Air Transport Command Base, where cargo aircraft ranging from the C-47 and C-54 of World War II fame to the following generations of heavy-lift transports, such as the Douglas C-118 Liftmaster, Boeing C-97 Stratofreighter, Douglas C-124 Globemaster and Lockheed C-141 Starlifter, were stationed. Muroc Army Air Field would be known as Edwards Air Force Base in honor of Captain Glenn Edwards, who lost his life while flight-testing the Northrop YB-49 flying wing near the desert base, then famous as *the* air force flight test and development center. The skies of San Bernardino County became home to almost every aircraft type imaginable. The contrails of jet fighters, bombers and transport jets, both commercial and military, would mark the beginning of the jet age. Experimental designs flying from Edwards AFB became common and, sometimes, tragic sights in county skies.

Small private aircraft filled the skies at lower altitudes, especially on the weekends, as pilots often flew to Big Bear Lake in the San Bernardino Mountains, east to Palm Springs or northeast to Las Vegas, Nevada. The sky was the limit, and it seemed limitless, too, in the halcyon days of the 1950s and '60s. Sky ranches, where a family could fly in and spend a night or two in a small cabin or camp on the ground under the wing of their aircraft, dotted the Mojave Desert. Airports that catered to private planes included Cable, Rialto, Morrow Field, Redlands, Big Bear, Chino, Apple Valley, Adelanto, Hesperia, Tri-City, Fontana Gilfillan, Riverview, Giant Rock, Yucca Valley and old San Bernardino Airport. Dozens of private and semiprivate strips dotted the Mojave Desert, along with those that had been built to support General George Patton's Eastern Mojave training "playground" during World War II. It was inexpensive in the second half of the twentieth century to fly, hunt, picnic or enjoy the great scenery of the legendary Mojave Desert with its rugged mountains and myriad dry lakes.

With the abundance of activity in the skies over the county, there were, of course, mishaps and accidents. Weather remained a primary factor, coupled with pilot error in most of the civilian losses, but there were a few cases of mechanical failure and some midair collisions, too. Military losses included pilot error and weather factors, but they also had a higher percentage of mechanical or systems failures. The very nature of military operational missions, training or otherwise, had risks that most civilian pilots do not experience or encounter in a lifetime of private flying. Military losses in San Bernardino County from 1946 until 2012 total nearly 159 aircraft with 126

Five USAF Douglas B-26 Invader light bombers crashed in San Bernardino County between 1947 and 1958. Two accidents were midair collisions, and two were weather related. The Douglas A/B-26 enjoyed a long operational career with the USAAF and USAF from 1944 until 1974. The photo depicts a USAF B-26C. *Photo courtesy AAHS.*

The October 29, 1947 crash site of USAF Douglas B-26C 44-34588 on south slope of San Sevaine Ridge, circa 1954. *Photo USAF Official via Bob Koch.*

aircrew and passenger fatalities. Civilian aircraft losses for the same period come to around 234, including 334 fatalities.

There were five USAF Douglas B-26 Invader accidents following World War II in San Bernardino County. The first occurred on October 29, 1947, when B-26C 44-34588 crashed on San Sevaine Ridge, killing all five aircrew members. The plane was flying from March AFB to Burbank in dense clouds that covered the entire Los Angeles basin and surrounding inland valleys. The burned wreckage was spotted the following day, and the remains of the crew were recovered on October 31. The crash site has been burned over in several wildfires since 1947, but it is overgrown by chaparral today.

The next B-26 loss happened in the extreme southwest corner of San Bernardino County in the Chino Hills where Orange and Riverside Counties share common borders with San Bernardino. This was another accident in which low stratus clouds blanketed the coastal plain and inland valleys, enveloping the hill and foothill areas of the San Gabriel and San Bernardino Mountains. Into this foggy blanket flew a USAF Douglas TB-26B 44-34636A, en route from Sheppard AFB in Texas via Williams AFB, Arizona, to Long Beach AFB. On the late afternoon of October 16, 1949, the TB-26B was observed flying into clouds east of the Chino Hills, and moments later, the aircraft flew through high-tension power lines near San Juan Hill, the highest point for miles around. The accident board found that the pilot had continued VFR (Visual Flight Rules) flight into IFR conditions with fatal results for all on board. The crash site is located in Chino Hills State Park, where small parts of 44-34636A can still be found.

The Douglas TB-26B Invader was utilized by the USAF in the late 1950s as a multi-engine trainer, target tug, transport or maid of all work. Five of these venerable veterans of World War II and the Korean War were assigned to fly from George AFB on a round-robin flight to Winslow and Phoenix in Arizona and then to Blythe, California, on January 31, 1958. As the formation headed east at 9:43 a.m., one of the TB-26 aircraft overran another, chopping off the tail assembly and causing the TB-26B to plunge into the desert, killing First Lieutenant Alexander Aros and Airman First Class Patrick W. Hughes. Both men were assigned to the Fourth Tow Target Squadron at George AFB. The TB-26B that collided with the doomed plane was itself badly damaged and was forced to make an emergency landing back at George AFB with the landing gear retracted. The tail assembly of TB-26B 41-39310 can still be seen in a remote area of the Mojave Desert north of Interstate 40 in the Old Dad Mountains, a place few people intentionally

The tail section of USAF TB-26B 41-39310 was chopped off in a midair collision over the Old Dad Mountains on January 31, 1958. *Photo by Rick Flarety.*

visit. The main impact of the TB-26B is a burn scar to the west of the tail assembly in an even more remote and desolate location.

The most dramatic and memorable accidents often involve midair collisions. The first such accident in the postwar period occurred on August 11, 1950, when four USAF Douglas B-26B Invader light bombers departed George Air Force Base on a night-formation training flight. Each B-26B had a flight crew of two officers on board. At about 9:15 p.m., while flying above El Mirage Dry Lake, two B-26Bs collided as they attempted to change positions within the formation. B-26B 44-34174 was torn apart and plunged into the desert, killing First Lieutenant Orvis L. Cureton and First Lieutenant William A. Brady Jr. The second B-26B 44-324677 crashed about a half mile from 44-34174, killing Captain Lyle N. Leavitt and critically injuring First Lieutenant Richard A. Barker. The collision occurred at approximately 11,500 feet, and the crews were apparently trapped in the spinning B-26s, except for First Lieutenant Barker, who managed to make a low-altitude bail out, suffering broken arms and legs because his parachute barely had time to open. Scattered debris from the ill-fated night-training flight still litters the crash area near El Mirage Dry Lake.

On May 2, 1951, two USAF Republic F-84E Thunderjets made a formation takeoff from George AFB and collided minutes later about ten miles north of the airbase. Fortunately, only one of the two aircraft involved crashed, and the pilot of that F-84E ejected successfully with only minor injuries.

Two USAF North American Aviation F-86F Sabre Jets on an operational training mission from Nellis AFB in Nevada collided at 8:22 a.m. over a remote area of eastern San Bernardino County on July 8, 1954. The collision occurred at twenty thousand feet, and F-86F 52-5098, flown by Second Lieutenant Charles W. Myers, exploded. He escaped using the ejection seat and landed in the desert in Mesquite Valley, sustaining minor injuries. Second Lieutenant James R. McCulloch, flying F-86F 52-5131, attempted to eject, but after several frantic attempts, he unfastened his seatbelt and was sucked out of the cockpit. He landed near Second Lieutenant Myers without injury. Both Sabre Jets shed parts over a wide area of desert and crashed within a quarter mile of each other near the rugged Clark Mountain Range. The air force removed most of the Sabre Jet wreckage, but unburned shiny aluminum parts can still be seen in this remote and pristine desert where mining activity once abounded.

Formation flying requires skill, and formation flying in jets requires the very best skills pilots have to offer. Flying formation at night can be very dangerous even for the best pilots. At 11:30 p.m. on November 18, 1954,

A deadly midair collision on the night of November 18, 1954, destroyed a trio of USAF North American Aviation F-86D Sabre Dogs and killed one of the pilots. *Photo USAF Official via Tony Accurso.*

three North American Aviation F-86Ds, the all-weather interceptor version of the famed F-86 Sabre series, collided at nine thousand feet, east of George AFB. The flight had departed Oxnard AFB at 10:55 p.m., following a practice intercept mission using a Strategic Air Command Convair B-36 bomber as the simulated target. At the time of the accident, the F-86D planes were returning to George, where they were assigned to the Air Defense Command (ADC).

F-86D 52-3732 was flown by First Lieutenant Archie F. Ridall Jr.; F-86D 51-5962 was piloted by First Lieutenant Karl D. Fechner; and First Lieutenant John K. Moser was the pilot of F-86D 51-5939. Regrettably, First Lieutenant Moser was killed, possibly striking part of his aircraft during an unsuccessful ejection. The two surviving pilots were unable to eject but managed to egress from their aircraft, both being sucked out of their cockpits by a vacuum effect. Once out of the cockpit, the pilots still had to pull the D-ring to deploy their parachutes. This collision is, thankfully, the one and only triple-midair event over San Bernardino County. The crash sites of the F-86Ds remain today on open space west of Bell Mountain, with two sites east of I-15 and one on the west side. All are microsites, but they remain as reminders of the hazards our air force pilots faced while providing for the peacetime defense of our nation.

In-flight refueling has been an important aspect of military aviation operations since the early 1950s. All USAF fighters and bombers are equipped to refuel in flight while engaged on long-range missions in both daylight and darkness. While midair collisions rarely occur during refueling operations, one did happen on July 7, 1964, at twenty-six thousand feet over the southern part of Death Valley National Park. The tanker aircraft was a Boeing KC-135A Stratotanker, 60-340. With a crew of four and 120,000 gallons of fuel on board, it was involved in a collision with single-seat Republic F-105D Thunderchief 61-091 at 7:58 a.m. The flaming wreckage of both aircraft rained down on and around Owlshead Dry Lake. None of the five USAF airmen were able to escape from their respective planes. Wreckage was scattered over several miles of rugged mountain terrain and the Owlshead Dry Lake, where it is still visible today. This was the second-worst aviation accident in the history of Death Valley National Park. The worst occurred on August 1, 1944, involving the collision of two B-24 Liberators that killed seventeen USAAF airmen.

The most famous midair collision over San Bernardino County occurred on June 8, 1966, during a photo session featuring five USAF and NASA aircraft that were powered by General Electric jet engines. This accident claimed the life of famed test pilot Joe Walker, who piloted the NASA Lockheed F-104N 57-813 Starfighter that collided with a USAF XB-70A 20207 Valkarie supersonic bomber. The XB-70A 20207 was flown by North American Aviation test pilot Al White, who ejected safely, but his copilot, USAF major Carl S. Cross, was unable to eject and died when the massive bomber impacted the Mojave Desert twelve miles north of Barstow. Crash sites of both the XB-70 and F-104N are located on private property, and small memorials honoring the memories of Mr. Walker and Major Cross were built there some years ago.

Civilian aircraft are not immune to midair accidents, as evidenced by the collision that occurred four miles southwest of Needles Airport. Two light planes were approaching to land on the early morning of March 15, 1977. An eastbound Beechcraft F-33A with two men on board collided with a westbound Mooney MK-20F with a solo pilot aboard. Both aircraft were in contact with the Needles Control Tower at the time of the accident, and both pilots were aware there was "other" traffic in the area. Sunrise might have been a factor in the tragic loss of three lives. The crash sites are located in a rugged area of hills and washes near two World War II–era training plane losses dating from 1942 and 1943.

Above: Dramatic photo taken moments before the collision between a NASA F-104N and massive USAF XB-70A on June 8, 1966, that destroyed both aircrafts and killed two of the three aircrew members involved. *Photo courtesy AAHS.*

Left: Memorial near XB-70A crash site honoring USAF major Carl S. Cross, the copilot of the XB-70A. *Photo by Ryan Gilmore.*

Memorial near F-104N crash site honoring noted USAAF World War II pilot and famous NACA/NASA test pilot Joseph A. Walker. *Photo by Sam Parker.*

July 27, 1979, was the date of a USMC midair crash near the Twenty-nine Palms Marine Corps Training Base. Two McDonnell F-4N fighter-bombers, Bu No 151413 and Bu No 152284, assigned to VFMA-321 collided while on a "routine" training mission northwest of the base airfield. All four crewmen ejected safely without serious injuries as their aircraft exploded and burned on a remote area of the base.

Two USAF McDonnell Douglas F-4E Phantom II fighter-bombers assigned to the Thirty-fifth Tactical Fighter Wing at George Air Force Base collided over the Mojave Desert north of Phelan in San Bernardino County on November 21, 1983. The training mission was to have simulated a low-altitude, two-plane surface-attack mission when something went terribly wrong, leading to the total destruction of both aircraft and the deaths of two crewmen aboard F-4E 75-00634. The crew of F-4E 75-00637 ejected successfully, sustaining moderate injuries. The collision occurred as the two jets were forming up before heading to a bombing and gunnery range. While the F-4Es carried no bombs, they were each armed with 2.75-inch rockets and one 20-millimeter nose-mounted M-61A1 rotary cannon. Some of these rockets and cannon rounds went off upon impact. The crash sites are located in an area of homes and small ranches, but thankfully, no homes were damaged and no residents injured. Scattered micro debris from the F-4Es is evident today in this rapidly growing high desert community.

Experimental, test and research aircraft had their share of accidents and mishaps across San Bernardino County in the 1950s, '60s and '70s. Not all of these losses involved manned aircraft. On September 10, 1953, a U.S. Navy Regulus I jet-powered cruise missile built by Vought Aircraft Corporation went off course and crashed twenty-five miles north of Barstow. Even though the Regulus I carried no explosives on board, it was specially instrumented and programmed to follow a prescribed course. A guidance malfunction caused the Regulus to crash, and because the design was classified at the time, a speedy recovery of the wreck was essential. Nonetheless, not all of the Regulus I was recovered, as Tony Accurso and his daughter Evelyn discovered when they located the crash site fifty-nine years later. Even as a microsite, the remnants of the Regulus constitute an important discovery for those interested in aircraft archaeology and aerospace accident history.

The loss of the USAF Bell X-2 6674 on September 27, 1956, in which Captain Melburn G. "Mel" Apt was killed while attempting to bail out following a successful speed run at 65,500 feet, made Captain Apt the first man to fly three times faster than sound. The X-2 rocket plane crashed south of Kramer Junction astride Highway 395. Although the X-2 wreckage has long since been removed, a memorial marker identifies the impact site and honors the service and sacrifice of Captain Apt.

Prior to the space shuttle, North American Aviation's X-15, of which three examples were built, was considered the most successful of all the manned rocket aircraft. Its defining contributions to aerospace science were its achievements in speed—4,520 miles per hour (Mach 6.6)—and altitude reaching—354,200 feet (69 miles above the earth). Many of the test pilots who flew the X-15 reached altitudes that qualified them for astronaut wings. The Edwards Flight Test Center motto, *Ad Inexplorata* (Toward the Unexplored), exemplified the X-15 test program that began in 1959 and came to a stellar close in 1968.

One air force test pilot, Major Michael J. Adams, earned his astronaut wings posthumously. While on his seventh mission piloting X-15 66672 on November 15, 1967, he reached an altitude of 266,000 feet and achieved a speed of Mach 5. Tragically, during the final stages of the test protocols, Captain Adams inadvertently entered into a hypersonic spin from which he could not recover, causing the X-15 to break up in flight and crash on the high desert north of the mining town of Johannesburg in northern San Bernardino County. Captain Adams was unable to eject from his stricken aircraft, possibly because he was incapacitated. He was killed instantly on impact.

The in-flight breakup of the X-15 occurred at such a high altitude that parts from 66672 rained down over many miles of desert and rugged mountains. Some of the wreckage included pieces of aircraft skin and structure that remained unrecovered until the 1990s, when the "X Hunters" and other groups began searching the flight path of the ill-fated X-15 on foot, in light aircraft and by balloon with a live-feed camera attached to it. Some of the parts of 66672 ended up in private collections, while others were given to the Edwards FTC History Office for preservation. The X-15 debris field was the most extensive until the space shuttle *Columbia* tragedy of February 1, 2003, that spread wreckage across more than three states.

In 2004, thanks to the efforts of John Bodylski of BSA Troop 323, who earned his Eagle Scout Merit Badge for the project, a permanent memorial marker honoring the service and sacrifice of Major Michael J. Adams was placed at the crash site. This project was completed with the approval of the Bureau of Land Management and members of the Adams family. It should be noted that Major Greg Frazier of civil air patrol Squadron 68 was an important contributor to the success of this project. Mr. Bodylski was also serving as a member of CAP Squadron 68 when the dedication ceremony was held on May 5, 2004. Present at the dedication were four members of the Adams family, NASA test pilot William Dana—a veteran of sixteen X-15 flights, including the final flight in the research program on October 24, 1968—as well as many interested aerospace aficionados. The color guard was provided by members of CAP Squadron 68. This was a day that I will never forget. The memorial plaque reads, in part, "In memory of his contribution: Major Michael Adams, USAF, the first in-flight fatality of the American Space Program." The memorial is accessible for public visitation via a dirt road four miles north of Highway 395 and a quarter mile west of the Trona Road at 35 25' 48" N by 117 35' 48" W. Visitors are asked to be respectful and leave no trace but their tire tracks.

Monuments and memorials great and small remind us of the losses sustained by our service men and women, but they are placed for civilian pilots, too. Some of these memorials exist in remote locations that take more than a day to reach in order to reflect and remember. Other markers exist only in the hearts and memories of those left behind, and these are no less poignant.

Left: Memorial plaque with flag honoring the service and loss of USAF major Michael J. Adams, who earned his Astronaut Wings posthumously on November 15, 1967, in the crash of North American Aviation X-15 66672. *Photo by G.P. Macha.*

Below: The venerable Douglas C-47D Skytrain served the USAAF and USAF for nearly forty years. Three USAF C-47D aircraft were lost in accidents in San Bernardino County, the best-known loss being that of 45-1124 on December 1, 1952, which killed thirteen military personnel. *Photo courtesy AAHS.*

Many World War II–era aircraft types continued to serve with our armed forces well into the 1950s, '60s and '70s. The longest serving were mostly transport or cargo aircraft. The venerable Douglas C-47 Skytrain and C-53 Skytrooper were also affectionately called "Gooney Birds," and they did not retire from military service in the United States until 1975. Over nine thousand of these aircraft were manufactured during the Second World War.

There were three fatal air force C-47 accidents in San Bernardino County following World War II. The first occurred on December 3, 1948, during a flight from Kirtland AFB in New Mexico to Muroc AFB in Kern County. The pilot of C-47D 43-48467 reported rain showers followed by clearing conditions as he approached Muroc. But darkness had fallen, and the Gooney Bird collided with the Kramer Hills some twenty-five miles east of Muroc, killing the four men on board. The pilot had reported seeing lights in the distance, but apparently, he could not see the rising terrain that lay ahead until it was too late.

The second C-47D accident was weather related, with darkness a compounding factor. On December 4, 1951, USAF transport 45-931A departed Norton AFB near the city of San Bernardino en route to Long Beach AFB with three passengers and a crew of two. The pilot was described as being in a hurry prior to departure from Norton with a copilot who had no C-47 flight experience. At 7:45 p.m., 45-931A collided with a rain- and cloud-obscured ridge above Day Canyon in the San Gabriel Mountains, near the community of Etiwanda. The weather and rugged topography hampered the recovery of all five victims until December 7 and 8.

The last of these Gooney Bird losses involved C-47D 45-1124, assigned to the Material Air Transport Command (MATS). On December 1, 1952, this aircraft departed Offutt AFB, Nebraska, on an administrative flight en route to March AFB in Riverside County, California. Two stops were made along the way, one at Roswell AFB, New Mexico, and the second at Davis-Monthan AFB, Arizona. Prior to departure from Davis-Monthan, the flight crew was apprised of a potentially difficult weather pattern affecting Southern California. The flight crew decided to proceed, and an IFR flight plan was filed. The departure was made at 7:25 p.m. with a complement of three air force flight crewmen and ten passengers: three air force, three marine, three army and one navy service member. The flight progressed normally until radio contact was lost at 9:57 p.m. Efforts to make radio contact with the crew of the C-47D continued for one hour without success. At the same time, the aircraft faded from the radar scope about twenty to twenty-five miles east of San Bernardino. A few hours later, 45-1124 was posted as missing, and a search was initiated the following morning.

The wreckage of the missing C-47D was spotted by a search aircraft from March AFB on December 4, 1952. The crash site was located on the east flank of 11,503-foot Mount San Gorgonio, the highest peak in Southern California. A ground rescue team was assembled for an overland trek from the Barton Flats area of the San Bernardino Mountains to the crash site. On December 5, an air force Sikorsky H-19A rescue helicopter managed to drop off an air force officer and staff sergeant near the C-47D wreckage, but heavy snow made it impossible to locate possible survivors or deceased personnel. Both air force men had to be taken off the mountain that same day, and a marine Sikorsky HRS-2 Bu No 129037 with an engine that developed one-hundred more horsepower than the H-19A was sent in for this perilous mission. With winds gusting to nearly sixty miles per hour, the pilot of the HRS-2 was forced to make a hard landing below the C-47D crash site near a place known as Mine Shaft Flat.

Then, there were three men on the mountain in below-freezing conditions, and the air force staff sergeant was suffering from frostbite. Meanwhile, a small ground team was following a tracked vehicle called the Weasel, and they too were struggling to reach the three men now stranded at Mine Shaft Flat. The weasel became bogged down in deep snow at Slushy Meadows, and the weather worsened rapidly. The marines sent another Sikorsky HRS-2, piloted by USMC captain Lud Tucker flying solo to save weight, managed to land and rescue the stranded trio and fly them safely back to March AFB. The ground team abandoned the Weasel and retreated to Barton Flats just as another snowstorm was arriving over the San Bernardino Mountains.

As the weather abated, the air force dispatched a forty-six-man ground team on December 16 to reconnoiter the C-47D crash site and recover bodies if possible. The elements proved to be too much for the team, the snow too deep and the temperatures too low. It was not until December 21 that four ground team members finally reached the crash site buried in snow so deep that only the C-47Ds tail and some wing sections were visible. The team did determine that the C-47D impacted the mountain approximately 200 feet below an 11,000-foot ridge and that most of the wreckage slid down to 10,100 feet MSL. The team retreated as yet another winter storm was about to arrive.

The fall and winter of 1952–53 was noted for a record snowfall in the San Bernardino Mountains, one that kept recovery teams at bay until mid-May 1953. It was only then that the grim task of recovering the dead could begin.

Two bodies were found in the tail area huddled together; both had sustained serious injuries and might have expired from a combination of shock and freezing temperatures. The body of one young marine, a private first class, was found a quarter mile below the main wreckage. His uniform jacket was turned up around his neck, and it was fully buttoned with his right arm extended. A full autopsy failed to show any internal trauma, broken bones or skull fractures. This young man survived the night, and perhaps into the next day. His arm was raised as if he were waving at search aircraft flying overhead.

The air force accident investigation board findings were that the cause of the accident could not be determined, but the "probable causes" were stated as follows: "inability of the pilot to determine his positive position at the Palm Springs Intersection due to weather, possible poor radio reception and a lack of adequate navigational aids at the Palm Springs Intersection." It was recommended that a very high frequency omni-directional range (VOR) be installed at Palm Springs to assist aircraft flying through the San Gorgonio Pass, and one was installed later as a result of the C-47D loss. It is important to note also that the C-47D was not equipped with radar, which would have made the looming mountain visible in the pilot's flight path. Today, powerful ground-based radars, transponders and the Global Positioning Satellite system have made flying in any weather, day or night, much safer.

I first visited the C-47D crash site in July 1963 while hiking overland from the summit of Mount San Gorgonio to Lodgepole Spring. At that time, there was no USFS trail passing through the site as there is today. My group from YMCA Camp Conrad and I were shocked to find personal effects, uniforms, caps, flight bags and a host of other items associated with the cockpit and passenger cabin. One wing was painted with a bright yellow X, a notice to aircraft flying nearby that this was a marked known crash site that need not be reported to the authorities. In later years after the Sky High Trail was built, hikers helped themselves to parts from the wreck, and gradually, the site was degraded, reduced and battered by rock falls and winter avalanches. The passage of sixty-one years has seen thousands of trekkers going by the remnants of C-47D 45-1124, but very few know the story of this tragic accident. In the summer of 2006, two memorial plaques were dedicated at the crash site with the approval of the USFS. The plaques were installed on a large boulder next to the trail through the combined efforts of George Bingham Jr. and his brother Harold Bingham, sons of Captain George F. Bingham, the pilot of the C-47D. Additional help was provided by Jarome Wilson of the San Gorgonio Wilderness Association, who played a key role in placing these

Above: The starboard wing and tail assembly minus the vertical stabilizer of USAF Douglas C-47D 45-1124. Note the cross painted on the wing to alert passing airmen or hikers that this was a known wreck that need not be reported as a missing aircraft. *Photo by G.P. Macha.*

Left: Memorial plaques were placed at the C-47D crash site in 2006, thanks to the efforts of Captain Bingham's sons and other volunteers. *Photo by P.J. Macha.*

memorial plaques, which include the accident date, type of aircraft involved and the names of those on board with their respective ages. The most senior man on board was a forty-seven-year-old air force chief warrant officer, and the youngest was eighteen. Captain Bingham was a married family man and a highly decorated B-17 pilot who earned the Distinguished Flying Cross while serving with the Eighth Air Force in England during World War II. He was thirty-five at the time of his death. I visited the C-47D site numerous times in the 1960s, and on each hike, I felt that I was at a place where time had suddenly and tragically stopped for the thirteen servicemen aboard 45-1124 on December 1, 1952.

The Fairchild C-82 Packet was ordered into production during World War II, but the war ended before it could be operationally deployed. In the postwar years, the C-82 was used to carry cargo and paratroops, but it was quickly supplanted by the larger and more powerful Fairchild C-119 Flying Boxcar. The air force declared the C-82 obsolete in 1954 partly because of an accident that occurred on September 21, 1954.

Fairchild C-82 45-57744 departed Norton AFB at 7:15 p.m. bound for Hill AFB, Utah. On board were four pilots, one flight engineer and three passengers. No cargo was being carried on this routine flight in which the three pilots on board were to receive flight instruction and passengers were to be delivered to Hill AFB. Norton AFB, now San Bernardino Regional Airport, is located near the base of the San Bernardino Mountains. Shortly after takeoff, the C-82 began its climb to cross the mountains near the community of Running Springs. Moments later, the right engine backfired and lost power. The instructor pilot, Captain Charles M. Eckstein Jr., USAF Reserve, immediately applied maximum power to the left engine while the unresponsive right engine remained at idle. Captain Eckstein ordered all passengers and crew to bail out as the C-82 was losing altitude over the mountainous terrain. No one on board was wearing a parachute; they were stored in the aft part of the fuselage. Frantically, the flight crew and passengers strapped on their parachutes and jumped. One airman froze at the door and had to be forcibly ejected, and by the time the last man had jumped, the left engine was smoking heavily. Unable to leave the flight deck, Captain Charles M. Eckstein became a hero pilot, staying with his ship until all on board had made their escapes. He did this at the expense of his own life.

Even though they landed in the rugged forested terrain of the San Bernardino National Forest, the eight men who parachuted to safety on the evening of September 21 sustained only minor injuries. Because darkness was falling, most of the survivors were not rescued until the next morning. The crash of the C-82 started a small forest fire, but it was quickly contained and extinguished on September 22. The remaining C-82s in USAF service were flown to disposition centers where they were scrapped or sold to corporations, mostly for use in the oil industry. The Stewart Davis Corporation of Long Beach, California, added a pod to the top of the C-82 fuselage with a jet engine inside. This modification helped give the C-82 another ten years of service life, but not with the USAF.

A postscript to this story is my unsuccessful searches to locate the C-82 crash site. Along with members of the Project Remembrance Team, we have made three trips into the accident area armed with reports, news articles and eyewitness statements in an effort to pay our respects to Captain Charles M. Eckstein Jr. and to honor his memory. The search will resume in the summer of 2013.

The Lockheed T-33A T-Bird was the first two-seat advanced jet trainer used by the USAF and USN. Almost six thousand were built. Ubiquitous at every air force base, it served not only as a trainer but also as a utility runabout. The T-33A served with the USAF from 1949 until the last NT-33A was retired in 1997. The T-bird was derived from the first fully operational jet fighter, the Lockheed P-80/F-80 Shooting Star. Six of these USAF T-Birds were lost in San Bernardino County, one of which crashed in the rugged Shadow Mountains on January 6, 1955. Tragically, both pilots were killed as they were making an instrument-approach landing at George AFB after a long cross-country flight from Perrin AFB in Texas that included a stop at Williams AFB, Arizona. Clouds obscured the mountains when the accident occurred at 1:40 p.m. The wreckage of T-33A 51-9115A lies scattered on both the north and south flanks of the Shadow Mountains because the pilot might have seen the ridge at the last second and pulled up, albeit too late.

Above old Route 66, now Interstate 15, in the Cajon Pass area of the San Bernardino Mountains, there was an aircraft wreck visible in the mid 1950s to motorists and passing aircraft. When I was eleven years old on a family trip to Colorado, my father pointed it out to me. After that, whenever we passed that way, I would look up on the mountainside to see it, but with the passage of time and at least one major forest fire, it was no longer visible. In 1965, I learned from a CAP pilot that this 1955 wreck was a navy Beechcraft SNB-4 Expeditor that had crashed in poor weather. That same year, I talked with a USFS ranger who recalled that the wrecked plane had twin rudders and was marked with yellow Xs and that three men had died in the accident. The ranger also advised me that the site was very difficult to reach because of locked gates, dense chaparral and steep terrain; he also confirmed the

Left: USN lieutenant Laskey Kirk Lacewell stands on the wing of an SNJ Texan during carrier qualifications in the Gulf of Mexico. *Photo USN Official via Kirk Lacewell.*

Below: Aerial view of USN Beechcraft SNB-4 Bu No 67260 on a mountain slope in the Cajon Pass. The accident occurred on January 9, 1955, killing three men on board. *Photo USN Official via AAIR.*

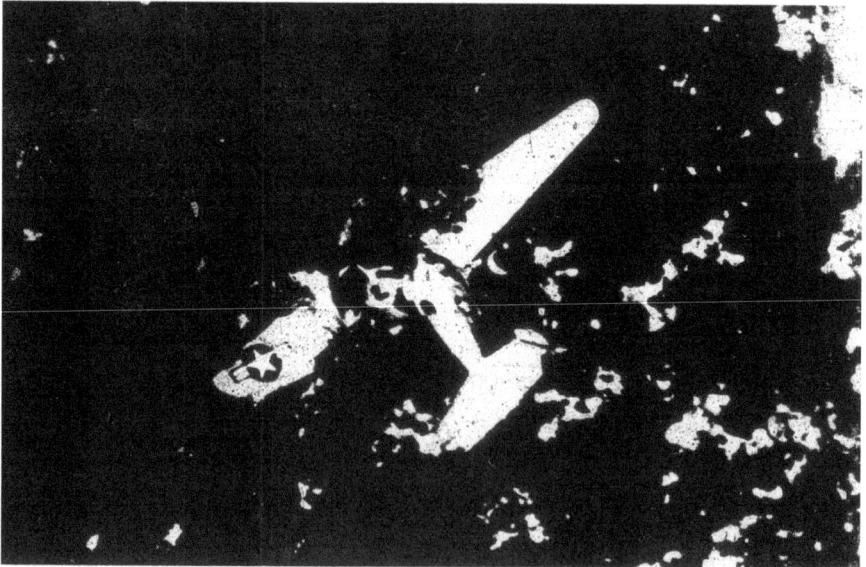

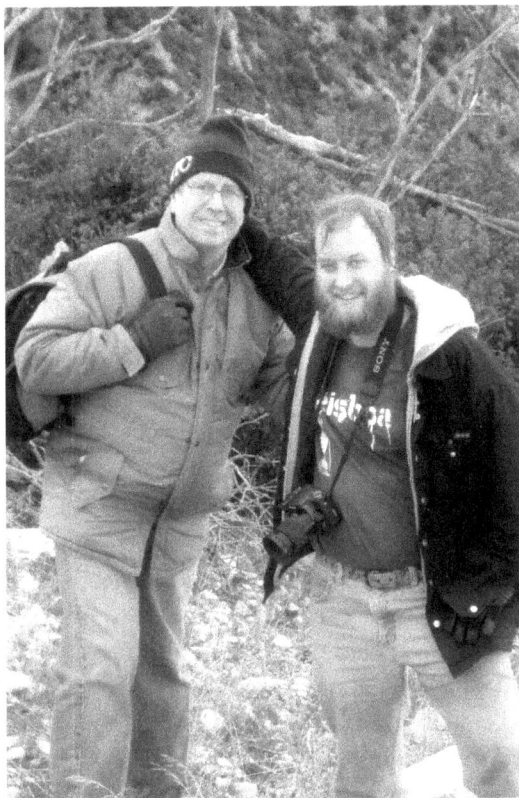

Kirk Lacewell and son Matt on December 4, 2010, after a strenuous day of hiking to pay their respects at the crash site of the SNB-4, where Kirk's father had died in January 1955. *Photo by G.P. Macha.*

year of the accident as 1955. At that time, lacking enough information, I decided to not attempt a crash site visitation.

Nevertheless, I continued my research efforts, and thanks to Craig Fuller at AAIR, I obtained an accident report that provided the accident date of January 9, 1955, and the aircraft type, Beechcraft SNB-4 Bu No 67260. Three navy men had been killed while on a night navigational training flight from a naval auxiliary air station in Monterey, California, to Norton AFB in San Bernardino County. Darkness and weather were listed as factors in this accident. I found more information about the exact location of the crash site thanks to a Bureau of Land Management surveyor who had stumbled on it. Even with the GPS position in hand, I made no plans to visit the site until I was contacted by Kirk Lacewell, the son of the copilot, Laskey Kirk Lacewell Jr., lieutenant, USN.

Kirk Lacewell wanted to visit his father's crash site with his son, Matt, to pay their respects, and he asked if our recently established Project Remembrance

Team would be able to facilitate the mission. Kirk's request was immediately approved, and planning for the visitation began. We notified the Forest Service, and it approved the mission for December 4, 2010, Lieutenant Laskey Kirk Lacewell's birthday. Kirk and Matt flew from their Florida home to nearby Ontario International Airport on December 3, and we were good to go the next day. A late fall storm was approaching Southern California, a day ahead of the forecasted arrival; this hastened our efforts to reach the SNB-4. Four-wheel-drive vehicles were used to negotiate the ridgeline road, from which we would descend one and a half miles on an old firebreak. Our hike required climbing, descending and then climbing again until we reached the point for the final descent to the crash site. With a tough seven hundred yards left to go, Kirk and I agreed to have Matt and the rest of the team press on. We were in radio contact throughout the remainder of the mission. The weather was ominous, the sky darkened and the winds increasing. But a moment later, the wind dropped, and a rainbow appeared. Seconds later, the radio crackled, "We found the plane." Matt Lacewell was at the site, and photos were being taken and prayers said. Our nation's flag was displayed, and tears were shed. The team honored those lost in the crash and saluted the courage of Kirk and Matt for completing their mission of respect and remembrance.

The hike out was arduous and cold, but we made it back to our vehicles at 4:15 p.m., reaching Interstate 15 shortly after dusk. That night, heavy rains fell across Southern California, and snow blanketed the San Bernardino Mountains, covering the wreckage of Bu No 67260. The SNB was another World War II–era aircraft still serving with the USN, USMC and the USAF as the C-45. Rugged and dependable, the Expeditor would continue to fly with our armed forces until late 1960s and early 1970s.

The North American Aviation B-25 Mitchell bomber was a World War II combat aircraft that found a niche in the jet age flying for the USAF as a multi-engine advanced trainer and staff transport. The last CB-25J staff transport was retired in 1960, but most of the B-25s were used for training. The last of these TB-25s were retired in 1959.

On January 26, 1956, TB-25N 44-86805, assigned to the USAF Air Training Command, was lost en route from Goodfellow AFB, Texas, to Norton AFB in San Bernardino, California, with four men on board. The TB-25N disappeared following confirmation by the pilot that he was west of the Palm Springs Intersection and that he would contact March AFB air traffic control (ATC) since the radar at Norton was not operational at that time. March ATC never established contact, and 44-86805 was posted as missing several hours later.

USAF North American Aviation TB-25 Mitchell similar to the TB-25N 44-86805 that crashed south of the Mount San Gorgonio summit on January 26, 1955, killing two crewmen and two passengers. *Photo courtesy AAHS.*

A search effort was launched on the morning of January 27 involving the USAF, CAP and the Sheriff Aviation Units of San Bernardino and Riverside Counties. The wreckage of the TB-25N was located by a search aircraft one week later on February 4. A ground team reached the crash site on the south flank of Mount San Gorgonio at 4:45 p.m. The ground team positively identified the wreckage as that of the missing TB-25N using the serial numbers on the tail of the demolished aircraft. The snow depth was described by San Bernardino County sheriffs' deputy Willard Farquhar as between eight and nine feet.

It would require several days to recover the bodies of the pilot, copilot and two airmen first class who were passengers on the ill-fated plane. Once that was accomplished, the wreck was left, undisturbed, to weather a succession of winter storms that would bury the wreckage until the late spring thaw. An air force team returned to the crash site in June 1956 to recover some personal effects and pilots' log books and to paint yellow Xs on the wings, fuselage and tail of the TB-25N.

The wreckage of 44-8605A is one of the least visited crash sites in the San Bernardino Mountains due in no small part to its location above nine thousand feet MSL, far from any hiking trails. In addition, the rugged, rocky

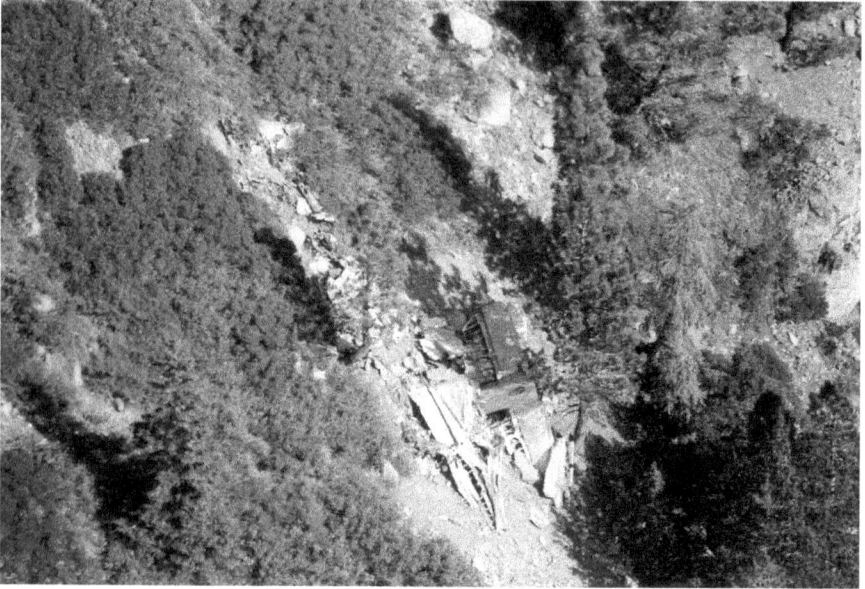

Aerial view of TB-25N crash site taken in November 2008. *Photo by G.P. Macha.*

The unburned and upside-down tail assembly of the TB-25N. *Photo by Todd Loiselle.*

terrain overgrown by buckthorn and manzanita makes it very difficult to reach. The TB-25N was on my list of the top ten yet-to-be-visited crash sites in California. Thanks to retired NTSB investigator and master pilot George Petterson, in November 2008, I was finally able to see the remains of this Mitchell bomber, albeit from the back seat of George's Piper PA-18 Super Cub. Armed with my best camera and telephoto lens, we made a number of standoff fly-bys that allowed me to document the crash site at a respectful distance.

The question of obtaining on-site photos at ground level still remained. In 2011, I asked expert mountaineer Todd Loiselle if he would make a one-day round-trip foray to the TB-25N. Todd accomplished this solo mission, using my aerial photos to plan his route. Since that time, only two other intrepid individuals have reached the crash site. One of them was Trey Brandt, a veteran wreck hunter from Arizona. For additional safety, Todd Losielle used the SPOT Personal Tracker, a satellite-based transmission system, for providing location-based information. In remote locations such as the TB-25N and many others, hikers often rely on "Mr. SPOT."

While many military accidents happen during routine flight operations, the loss of Lockheed JF-104A 55-2962 on May 1, 1957, was anything but routine. The F-104 Starfighter was nicknamed the "missile with a man in it" because of its stubby razor-sharp wings that measured a total of twenty-one feet, eleven inches. Within the fifty-four-foot, nine-inch fuselage was a powerful General Electric J-79 turbojet engine that propelled the Starfighter to world speed, time to climb and altitude records during the mid- to late 1950s. Speeds of up to 1,404.19 miles per hour and altitudes of up to 91,249 feet were achieved, but not without a cost in lives and aircraft. Most USAF pilots called the F-104 the "Zipper" because the F-104's ejection-seat escape system, powered at high speeds by a 20-millimeter cannon shell, could not clear the T-tail. Therefore, the seat fired downward; this was effective at altitude, but not during takeoffs and landings.

On May 1, 1957, John J. "Jack" Simpson was the Lockheed Company test pilot flying JF-104A 55-2962 assigned to perform a series of tests at twenty-seven thousand feet consisting of one-gravity stall approaches and side slips; however, the mission was scrubbed early because one of the test instruments on board was not working properly. Mr. Simpson was flying back to Air Force Plant 42 at Palmdale Airport when he reported the right aileron was deflected upward. As he started his descent, the JF-104A pitched violently downward, to which Mr. Simpson responded by pulling full aft stick. The controls failed to respond, and he was forced to eject at seventeen

Above: The Lockheed F-104A Starfighter, capable of speeds over one thousand miles per hour and often described by numerous nicknames, including "the missile with a man in it" and the "Zipper." *Photo courtesy AAHS.*

Left: Lockheed Aircraft Company test pilot John J. "Jack" Simpson about to climb aboard F-104A 55-2955. *Photo courtesy Mr. John J. Simpson.*

Opposite: Pat J. Macha in the impact crater made by Jack Simpson's F-104A 55-2962. *Photo by G.P. Macha.*

thousand feet while traveling at 380–400 miles per hour. As Mr. Simpson was descending safely by parachute, his JF-104A crashed and exploded on the Mojave Desert north of Highway 58, northeast of Kramer Junction. As a side story, just a few days earlier Mr. Simpson had another emergency, and he made a successful dead-stick (engine-out) landing at Palmdale Airport in a YF-104A 55-2955, from which he walked away with only bumps and bruises.

Jack "Suitcase" Simpson was no stranger to danger. During the Korean War, he flew sixty-one combat missions in the F-80 Shooting Star and the F-86F Sabrejet, which he named "Suitcase's Appleknocker." Following his May 1 ejection from the JF-104A, he elected to seek work elsewhere, and he was promptly hired as a test pilot for North American Aviation, where he flew test missions in the F-100 Super Sabre. I interviewed Suitcase Simpson on several occasions about his flying career and his many close calls as a test pilot. I was surprised to learn that Mr. Simpson had never seen the official copy of his JF-104A accident report, nor did he know where his Starfighter had crashed on the Mojave Desert. Because of his interest, a copy of the report was obtained, and thanks to a team effort, we were able to locate the crash site of 55-2962 and provide both the report and site photos to Suitcase. He thanked me and wanted me to know that he had lost many friends testing the F-104A and that a total of twenty-one pilots had been killed flying the earliest version of the Starfighter.

After modifications, the F-104C became an effective fighter-bomber for the USAF and a safer aircraft, too, because the rocket-powered seat fired upward. There were fourteen F-104A and F-104C crashes in San Bernardino County, with four C models clustered around Cuddeback Dry Lake, once used as a USAF bombing and gunnery range. The last F-104C in USAF service was retired in 1975, but the type continued with NASA until 1994.

U.S. Navy and marine accidents were not uncommon across San Bernardino County. There were ten Douglas A-4 Skyhawk losses, the first of which killed famed Douglas Company test pilot James B. "Jimmy" Verdin on January 13, 1955. Verdin was a highly decorated World War II naval aviator who earned both the Navy Cross and the Distinguished Flying Cross. He was promoted to the rank of lieutenant commander, and following his retirement from the navy, he joined Douglas Aircraft, achieving fame for flight testing the F4D-1 Skyray, in which he set a world speed record on October 3, 1953. Following his contributions to the F4D-1 program, he was assigned to the A4D-1 test program. The A-4 was designed by Ed Heinemann, and the Skyhawk earned nicknames such as Heinemann's Hot Rod, Bantan Bomber, Mighty Mite and the Scooter. The A-4 enjoyed continuous production from 1954 to 1979, and it still serves in a number of foreign air forces and navies to the present day.

Flight-testing prototypes of any new design can be hazardous, as test pilots are asked to analyze flight characteristics in every possible envelope—speed, maneuvering, systems analysis—at all altitudes, including the designed maximum and down on the deck, a few yards off the ground. On January 13, 1955, Jimmy Verdin was piloting a protoype Skyhawk, Bu No 137815, when he encountered violent vibrations caused in part by aileron flutter at high speed, forcing Verdin to eject. His parachute failed to open, and he was killed. Bu No 137815 crashed on the Mojave Desert southeast of Kramer Hills and east of highway 395. A large crater is still visible at the crash site with scattered debris covering several hundred yards of open ground. The Verdin accident was witnessed by a USAF pilot Captain Mel Apt while he was flying a chase plane mission for a different test aircraft. Ironically, eight months later, Captain Apt would be killed on September 27, 1956, while flying the Bell X-2. The wreck of the X-2 and the A4D-1 crash are separated by only four miles.

There is no shortage of diverse topography in San Bernardino County, including the Pisgah Crater, lava flow and Lavic Dry Lake, all of which are adjacent landforms located just south of Interstate 40 and west of the small community of Ludlow. Interestingly, there are two unrelated A-4 Skyhawk wrecks on the lava flow. I have visited both crash sites in recent years. One loss

Left: Tom Maloney and G. Pat Macha at the tail section of McDonnell Douglas A-4M Skyhawk Bu No 160038, which crashed on the Pisgah lava flow on May 10, 1982, following successful pilot ejection. *Photo by P.J. Macha*.

Below: On the Pisgah lava flow, Pat J. Macha holds a wing section of A-4M Bu No 160038 with star-and-bar insignia. *Photo by G.P. Macha*.

is a USMC McDonnell/Douglas A-4M Bu No 160038 assigned to VMA-311 at El Toro MCAS. The pilot was making strafing runs over the gunnery range on the Twenty-nine Palms Marine Corps Base when he experienced loss of power; after several attempted engine restarts, he was forced to eject on the morning of May 10, 1982. The pilot, a marine major, made a hard landing on the lava flow and sustained a broken leg. He was picked up by a USMC helicopter within thirty minutes and flown to the base hospital.

The second A-4 loss on the lava flow was an earlier version of the Skyhawk and, initially, a mystery because we did not know the bureau number, pilot's name or accident date. Researching all of the A-4 losses in the Ludlow area paid off when one of the reports described an A-4C Bu No 148570 assigned to Navy Squadron VA-65 that crashed on August 18, 1966. The surname on the accident report, Tyszkiewic, grabbed my immediate attention because I had taught high school with Mr. Charles Tyszkiewic, and when I called him, he confirmed the pilot in question was indeed his brother. As with the May 1982 A-4M loss, an engine flameout following a strafing run resulted in unsuccessful attempts at a restart of the turbojet engine, and Lieutenant Commander Arthur Kasimir Tyszkiewicz was forced to eject at 2,500 feet above ground level (AGL), landing without injury as his crippled Skyhawk crashed and exploded nearby. Tragically, on January 14, 1967, Lieutenant Commander Tyszkiewic lost his life following a midair collision over Laos during the height of the Vietnam War. Although he ejected successfully and parachuted into the jungle, when the rescue helicopter tried to recover him, the cable became entangled, and he was dropped back into the jungle with fatal results. Lieutenant Commander Tsyzkiewicz was thirty-three at the time of his death.

Another mystery A-4 crash site was located following a search flight with George Petterson in August 2009 over the Bristol Mountain, a rugged and barren desert range north of Ludlow. Seeing the wreckage was one goal achieved, but confirming the aircraft type on the ground had to wait until cooler weather arrived that fall. In November, our ground team reached the scattered remains of a navy Douglas A-4C Bu No 148520 assigned to VA-34 that had crashed as the result of a midair collision with another aircraft. Fortunately, only one A-4 was lost; the other A-4, a navy B model, landed safely after flying to China Lake NOTS. We located a pilot's name painted below the canopy that did not match the name in the report, but it was not unusual for one aircraft to be flown by a number of different pilots. Happily, the pilot of Bu No 148520 ejected safely and sustained only minor injuries. Today, the crash site is largely undisturbed because of its difficult-to-reach location.

The wreckage on the Pisgah lava flow of USN Douglas A-4C Bu No 148570 that crashed on August 18, 1966, following successful pilot ejection. Note the intact horizontal stabilizers in the center of the debris field. *Photo by G.P. Macha.*

Chris LeFave holds a section of the rudder from USN A-4C Bu No 160038 on the Pisgah lava flow. *Photo by G.P. Macha.*

Tail section from Piper PA-31 that crashed on January 14, 1979, while attempting a takeoff from a remote airstrip near the Hart Mine Road in the Lanfair Valley. *Photo by G.P. Macha.*

The crash of the aforementioned A-4s, a 1942 B-24D (see chapter two), a civilian Beechcraft BE-35 Bonanza that killed three persons on July 6, 1964, the fatal loss of a navy McDonnell F-4B Phantom II on June 6, 1965, followed by a nonfatal loss of an air force F-4D Phantom II on July 8, 1968, and then the fatal nighttime crash of an alleged drug-running Piper Apache on June 6, 1984—all of which were near Ludlow—gave rise, in some aviation circles, to the notion that a "Ludlow Triangle" existed, in which aircraft and their crews became discombobulated and crashed. This bit of folklore is of course utter nonsense.

Three other aircraft wrecks associated with illegal activities can still be seen on the Eastern Mojave Desert, and two of these are Piper PA-31 Navajo twin-engine six-to-eight-seat lightplanes. The first crashed in a failed takeoff attempt from a remote desert airstrip near the Ivanpah Road on January 14, 1979. The second crashed on June 2, 1984, in a landing attempt south of Baker and east of the Kelbaker Road, killing its two occupants. Both of these wrecks remain highly visible to this day.

We lose good people, too, in aviation accidents while trying to help or save others. The civil air patrol, San Bernardino Sheriffs' Aviation Unit, San Bernardino County Fire Department, air tankers contracted to the U.S. Forest

Service and the U.S. Military have all sustained losses of personnel and aircraft. When the lives of first responders are lost, it is especially heartbreaking.

Cajon Pass and the surrounding mountains have snared many civilian and military aircraft mostly in bad weather or darkness. On the evening of September 12, 1976, a Sikorsky S-55 on a medical emergency flight collided with power lines near Cleghorn Road, killing all four persons on board. Another medical emergency flight loss occurred on April 17, 1988, when an Aerospatiale AS355F struck a power line and crashed in rainy weather, killing the pilot and nurse, although the patient being transported survived. He was found by rescuers sitting in a creek bottom; his survival was attributed to the fact that he had been securely strapped to a full body board at the time of the accident.

The risks that first responders face do not necessarily diminish with improved technology and training, as evidenced by the loss of a Bell 222U on September 7, 2002, while it responded at night to an emergency call from the California Highway Patrol on Interstate 15 to a vehicle accident near the town of Baker. The 222U had departed Parhump, Nevada, with a crew of three on board. The crew radioed at 4:20 a.m. that they were about three minutes out, but by 4:30 a.m., the helicopter had crashed and exploded on the desert, killing the pilot, flight nurse and paramedic. An extensive investigation by the NTSB revealed possible main rotor separation prior to impact. The crash site is located west of State Line, Nevada, in San Bernardino County near Interstate 15. Three memorial crosses mark the crash site, each bearing the first name of the heroic crew.

The next tragic EMS accident happened on the night of December 10, 2006, after a patient was taken to the hospital in Loma Linda, and the helicopter, a Bell 412SP, was returning to its base on the high desert with a pilot and two medical crew members on board. Fog obscured the upper reaches of the Cajon Pass when the helicopter collided with terrain near Oak Hills, killing all three crew members. During a visit in January 2009, George Petterson and I noted three separate memorials marking the crash site. One is a stately cross overlooking the site, and two other monuments of rocks, mementos, small parts of the Bell 412SP, flags, signs, a statue of an angel and crosses adorn the hallowed ground where the gallant crew died. It is not possible to visit any of these memorial sites and not be moved.

Celebrity accidents always receive extensive press coverage. The flight of a chartered Lear Jet was to have been routine for a captain and first officer sent to Palm Springs Municipal Airport on Thursday, January 6, 1977, to fly Mrs. Natalie "Dolly" Sinatra and her friend Mrs. Anthony Carbone to Las Vegas, Nevada, to see Frank Sinatra's opening performance at Caesar's

Place. The Lear Jet Model 24B N12MK departed on Runway 30 at 4:55 p.m. and climbed rapidly to nine thousand feet, traveling at an estimated 375 miles per hour. All appeared to be going well, except that the pilots aboard N12MK failed to execute a right turn shortly after departure that would place them on a heading to Las Vegas. Instead, they remained on a northwesterly track toward the towering San Bernardino Range that they could not see in the clouds and gathering winter darkness.

At 5:00 p.m., the Lear Jet impacted the high terrain of Ten Thousand Foot Ridge in the San Gorgonio Wilderness. The flight crew and its passengers died instantly, as N12MK disintegrated, scattering wreckage over a half-mile area. There was almost no post-impact fire, as the fuel vaporized, creating a brief flash of light over the snow-covered ridge. Moments later, air traffic control realized what had happened to the Lear Jet, and the San Bernardino County Sheriffs' Department was called into action. The suspected crash area could not be searched because of heavy snowfall on January 7 and 8, but a helicopter was able to spot wreckage on Sunday, January 9. Deputies were taken to the crash site by helicopter, where they found the going difficult in snow more than four feet deep. Low temperatures and high winds prevented the deputies from spending the night, but they returned the next day to begin the grim task of recovering the remains of those on board N12MK. The National Transportation Safety Board investigation concluded that a combination of factors contributed to the accident, including miscommunication between the flight crew and the controller and inattentiveness on the part of the flight crew and controller, who should have noted that the Lear Jet failed to make the right turn at the appropriate intersection to assume the Las Vegas destination heading.

Few people have hiked Ten Thousand Foot Ridge—a forested, rugged area that is bounded on the east by Hell for Sure Canyon and on the west and south by the North Fork of the Whitewater River Canyon. Lake Peak and Fish Creek Meadows mark the northwest and northeasterly boundaries. Curious about what remained at the Lear Jet crash site, I asked Todd Loiselle if he would consider a mission to locate and photo document N12MK. In the summer of 2010, Todd found the widely scattered wreckage of the blue-and-white jet that had carried four people to a tragic death on January 6, 1977.

Another accident involving a celebrity occurred on March 21, 1987, when the son of singer and movie star Dean Martin was killed while flying a California Air National Guard McDonnell Douglas F-4C Phantom 64-0923. Captain Dean P. Martin and his crewman, Captain Ramon Ortiz, were lost while flying a routine mission from March AFB. The crash site,

Todd Losielle holds a section of the control surface from Lear Jet Model 24B N12MK on the remote and seldom-visited Ten Thousand Foot Ridge. *Photo courtesy Todd Loiselle.*

Wreckage from the January 6, 1977 crash of N12MK that includes an oval passenger-window frame. *Photo courtesy Todd Loiselle.*

93

while located in the San Bernardino Mountains, was not in San Bernardino County, but in neighboring Riverside County. Weather and darkness were factors in this tragic accident.

A Lear Jet accident occurred in San Bernardino County on December 23, 2003, when a Model 24B N600XJ crashed, killing the captain and first officer southeast of Helendale on rocky desert lands. The aircraft was en route from Chino Airport to Sun Valley, Idaho, to pick up passengers when it pitched nose down at twenty-four thousand feet and dove almost vertically into the ground. In an effort to identify the cause of the accident, 100 percent of the wreckage was recovered for evaluation. The impact crater was forty-three feet long by seventeen feet wide, and the crater was between twenty-four inches and thirty inches deep. The National Transportation Safety Board determined that "there was a loss of aircraft control for undetermined reasons." The cause of this accident remains a mystery to this day.

Whenever a beloved member of a family dies suddenly and tragically, it can be overwhelming for those left behind. No matter how the grieving process goes, there are often long-term problems that arise for the survivors, especially for the children of the deceased. The facts about every aircraft accident are just one part of the story. These facts and findings are archived by the Federal Aviation Administration, National Transportation Safety Board and its predecessor, the Civil Aeronautics Board (CAB), but for those left behind, they are kept in the most private places of the heart.

I was contacted in 2007 by Jeff Corder about an air crash that claimed his father's life on June 7, 1964. Jeff wanted to visit the crash site to pay his respects to his best friend and beloved father, Rex C. Corder, who was the pilot of the Beechcraft Model 95 Travel Air, N2055C. Also on board were businessman Curtis F. Turrill and attorney Ray E. Snodgrass. The flight had originated in Bend, Oregon, with an en route stop at Reno, Nevada, before proceeding to Ontario Airport in San Bernardino County, the final destination. The weather on the final leg of the flight required an IFR flight plan that Rex Corder was highly qualified to follow. As N2055C approached the San Bernardino Mountains, a radar approach control (RAPCON) controller at March AFB instructed Mr. Corder to assume a new heading that would take him away from his destination. Mr. Corder asked the controller to repeat and verify the new heading that he had been assigned. The new heading did not seem to be a good idea to Mr. Corder, but choosing not to follow the controller's instructions was an option that pilots rarely acted on. They are trained to follow the directives of those in authority, at times to their great peril. Just minutes later, while on the compass heading

120 degrees, as assigned by the RAPCON controller, N2055C flew into the northwest shoulder of 10,649-foot San Bernardino Peak with fatal results for all three men on board.

The Travel Air collided with trees before smashing into a steep rocky slope, where it burst into flames at 2:55 p.m. The crash was heard in nearby Angelus Oaks, a small community astride Highway 38, where a resident immediately notified the sheriffs' department. Because clouds obscured the mountains, it was not possible to see the accident site. It was not until late that night that Lieutenant Willard Farquhar of the SBCSD and USFS firefighters arrived at the crash scene, where they worked to contain and extinguish the post-impact fire that had consumed the center section of the Travel Air and burned trees nearby. At dawn on June 8, the wreckage was positively identified as that of N2055C, and the sad task of contacting the next of kin began. Unfortunately, radio stations got the word out before the families received official notification.

The Civil Aeronautics Board investigation concluded that the loss of N2055C and those on board was the result of controller error in which the pilot was misidentified and misdirected. Weather was cited as a compounding factor. The FAA and the CAB recommended that all aircraft be equipped with a transponder that would make it easier for radar controllers to identify the aircraft that they were responsible for. Transponders were a new technology item in 1964. Ironically, Rex Corder had told friends he planned to install one in his Travel Air within a few months. Sadly, he never had a chance to.

On August 26, 2007, members of the Project Remembrance Team escorted Jeff Corder and his nephew Chris Dillard to the crash site of the airplane Jeff had flown in as a child. Thunderstorms had been forecast for the day of the hike, but they failed to materialize. We enjoyed the shade provided by cumulus clouds, ponderosa, sugar pines and Jeffery pines. As the team entered the debris field of the Travel Air, everyone was affected in some way as we climbed toward the point of impact together. Feelings ran the gamut from empathy and compassion for what Jeff was going through to hope that closure and peace of mind would be Jeff's at day's end. There were tears shed and prayers said for the victims of the crash by members of the group, who only a few days before had been strangers but were now friends. A small memorial plaque was placed, photos were taken and the wreckage was examined quietly and respectfully. We had touched the past together, where time stopped for three friends on June 7, 1964.

On July 27, 2013, members of the Project Remembrance Team returned to the Travel Air crash site with Jeff Corder and his cousin Dell Corder.

Jeff Corder sits with the wing section from Beechcraft Travel Air N2055C following a long hike to honor his beloved father's memory. *Photo by P.J. Macha.*

Bob Turrill, the eldest son of passenger Curtis F. Turrill, brought his son Steven. Rick Snodgrass, son of passenger Ray E. Snodgrass, bought his wife, Margaret, and their grandson Karl. Tom Maloney, Bruce Guberman, David Lane, my son and I provided guidance, support and assistance for the families. We salute the courage and determination shown by all of the family members as they climbed more than 1,200 vertical feet to pay their respects to those they loved, admired and lost on June 7, 1964.

A Beechcraft Model 35 Bonanza crashed on June 6, 1964, just off of I-40 near the tiny desert hamlet of Ludlow, killing a family of three who were en route from Long Beach, California, to Boulder City, Nevada. High winds were a factor in this accident as the pilot tried in vain to make an emergency landing at a small airstrip parallel to the highway.

While some pilots might be unfortunate, others seem to lead charmed lives. This was certainly the case for Henry "Hank" Stegman, who was well known in Huntington Beach and at the old Meadowlark Airport (now a shopping center and housing tract), where he kept his Mooney MK20C, N6423U. Hank especially liked to fly his Mooney to Big Bear City Airport, located high in the San Bernardino Mountains, where he also owned a cabin. During the holiday season of 1976, he flew to Big Bear the day after Christmas to spend some quality quiet time until his planned return to Meadowlark on December 31, New Years Eve.

Hank made an easterly departure from Big Bear City Airport at 7:00 a.m. in clear but very cold conditions. Since the airport had no control tower, there were no witnesses to his takeoff. Less than a minute after liftoff, Hank was in serious trouble as his windshield had completely iced over. Not being able to see where he was going, he used his instruments to maintain level flight as he tried to clear the windshield and return to the airport. As he made a turn to the left, he clipped a tree that spun his Mooney around so that as he crashed, the tail and empennage of his aircraft absorbed all of the impact energy. When his plane came to rest, Hank opened his cockpit door and saw that he had crashed on a ridge northeast of the airport. He turned off his fuel and electrical switches, got out of the plane and discovered that he had sustained no injuries whatsoever. So Hank simply gathered a few belongings and hiked back to his cabin, where he turned the heat back on and made coffee.

Several hours later, another pilot departing Big Bear City Airport spotted the wrecked Mooney and radioed the authorities. The San Bernardino County Sheriffs' Department sent sheriff deputies to the crash scene, and of course, they were mystified as to what had transpired. Checking the paperwork in the Mooney, the deputies determined that Henry Stegman was the pilot and that he had a cabin nearby. Ten minutes later, they were knocking on Hank's cabin door. The officers were invited in, and Hank told his story. "Have you been drinking, Mr. Stegman?" asked the officers. Hank answered, "Coffee yes, alcohol no," and then he was soundly chastised for not reporting his accident to the authorities.

Hank continued to fly for many uneventful years until he passed away from natural causes. N6423U was salvaged for its radio and instruments, landing gear and engine parts. Eventually, most of the aluminum was removed by salvagers, and the incident was forgotten until Big Bear resident and avid hiker Dave Trimble stumbled on the airplane wreckage and reported it to me. My son and I were able to visit the crash site in December 2005. It was not until we saw parts that the accident site could be identified as that of Hank Stegman's Mooney Mk20C.

Even luckier than Hank Stegman were two men flying a Cessna 172N N6443E on February 20, 2009. They were en route from San Bernardino International Airport to Big Bear City Airport when they started to gain altitude as they flew into rising terrain. Realizing too late that they did not

Left: Pat J. Macha holds a piece of the Mooney MK 20 lightplane that Hank Stegman crashed following takeoff from Big Bear Airport on December 31, 1976. Mr. Stegman sustained only minor injuries in the crash that destroyed his aircraft. *Photo by G.P. Macha.*

Below: Aerial view of Cessna 172N N6443E from which two men walked away without serious injuries. *Photo by G.P. Macha.*

Opposite: Ground view of N6443E in forested area near Rim of the World Highway. *Photo by P.J. Macha.*

have the power or time to maneuver out of the situation, the pilot was forced to make a split-second decision. His combination of luck and skill saved two lives by successfully crash-landing in rugged mountainous terrain. The injuries were minor, and both men were rescued by San Bernardino County Sheriffs' helicopter following a distress call. At a later date, the aircraft owner returned to the 172N and removed instruments and radio, leaving the mostly intact aircraft where it remains today. Thanks to Chris LeFave's aerial search efforts, N6443E was located, and soon after, Chris was able to visit the abandoned Cessna. Thanks to George Petterson and his Super Cub, I was able to view the crash site from air, and later, Chris escorted my son on foot to one of the few aircraft wrecks visible on Google Earth, if you know where to look that is.

The very nature of all training and flying can sometimes make flight operations problematic, but advances in aerospace technology and training procedures continue to improve, and as a result, our loss rates are a fraction of those in the 1950s, '60s and '70s. The sky is no longer the limit as we stand on the threshold of commercial travel into space in the twenty-first century.

CHAPTER FOUR
THE MISSING

How They Haunt Us

Aircraft flying over San Bernardino County have vanished without an apparent trace. Sometimes extensive ground and air search efforts have come to naught despite hundreds of flight hours by air force, civil air patrol and the San Bernardino County Sheriffs' Aviation Unit.

The case of USAF Reserve pilot Second Lieutenant Gordon L. Zempel, who disappeared on January 24, 1948, while on a routine training flight from San Bernardino Air Force Base (renamed Norton AFB in 1950), was a mystery for nearly eight months.

Gordon L. Zempel graduated from San Bernardino High School in June 1942. In December of that year, he applied for aviation cadet training with the U.S. Army Air Force. He was inducted the following January, having just turned eighteen. After spending seven months with the Ninety-seventh College Training Detachment, he was assigned to Santa Ana Army Air Base in Orange County, California, where his preflight training began. In December 1943, Aviation Cadet Zempel commenced primary flight training in the Boeing Stearman PT-17 "Kaydet" at the Rankin Aeronautical Academy near Tulare, California. By February 1944, he was flying the Vultee BT-13A Valiant basic trainer at Gardner Field near Taft, California. From there, Aviation Cadet Zempel went on to advanced training in the twin-engine Cessna AT-17 Bobcat in Stockton, California. On June 27, 1944, he was commissioned as a flight officer, a rank approved by President Roosevelt to accommodate the demand for pilots who did not have at least two years of college prior to commissioning.

In the summer of 1944, Flight Officer Zempel was assigned to Victorville Army Air Field, where he flew the Beechcraft AT-11 Kansan on bombardier training missions. Later, he was assigned to Boeing B-17 transition training in New Mexico and, finally, to a base in Texas, where he was released from active duty in December 1945. Because Gordon Zempel wanted to continue to serve his country and to continue to fly, he applied for a commission as a second lieutenant in the army air force reserve. In January 1947, he was appointed to the reserve officer corps and was assigned to the San Bernardino Air Force Base, from where his ill-fated last flight would originate.

Second Lieutenant Zempel was scheduled to fly a solo proficiency-training mission not to exceed two hours on January 24, 1948. The aircraft he was assigned to fly was a North American AT-6D Texan, the famed World War II advanced trainer flown by the air force, navy and marines. Takeoff from San Bernardino Air Force Base was made at 8:52 a.m. in good weather. Second Lieutenant Zempel had accrued 767 flight hours, and he was instrument rated, too. After one hour of flying, the young pilot returned to the San Bernardino Base and requested permission to continue flying locally for one additional hour. At 1:15 p.m., he was posted missing, and a search was initiated by the air force. The San Bernardino County Sheriffs' Department was notified, as was the California civil air patrol, the National Guard and the Ninth Search & Rescue Squadron at March AFB. Since this was to have been a local flight, no formal flight plan was filed, but the San Bernardino Mountains were placed high on the list of places where Second Lieutenant Zempel might have gone.

Within two days of the disappearance, a heavy snowfall blanketed the mountains, hampering both aerial and ground efforts. Around 170 search missions were flown within the first two weeks without success. Ground teams on skis and snowshoes scoured the area around Big Bear Lake as more winter storms slammed the region, finally bringing all search efforts to a halt. Notices to airmen were posted alerting anyone flying over, around or near the San Bernardino Mountains and the Cajon Pass that a USAF T-6D Texan aircraft, serial number 42-85065, was missing with one man on board. The T-6D was described as unpainted, natural aluminum clearly marked with USAF insignia. Dozens of reports were made by pilots who had seen aircraft wreckage in Cajon Pass, near Crestline and south of Big Bear Lake, but these sightings all proved to be old wrecks and not the missing AT-6D.

The Zempel family hoped and prayed their beloved Gordon would be found alive within the first few days of his disappearance, but after two weeks, hope faded that he could survive winter's deep snows and low temperatures. The snow pack melted late in the spring and early summer of 1948, and the search teams knew it was time to fly the deep canyon recesses, dense forests, mountain peaks and ridges. Reports continued to come in about plane wrecks above Devore, another on Moon Ridge, and near the tiny hamlet of Seven Oaks, but these all proved to be old wrecks. Then, on August 6, 1948, Lieutenant Albert W. Homza, a pilot from the Ninth Search & Rescue Squadron, spotted the missing Texan trainer because of a parachute billowing in the breeze. Later that same day, a ground team guided by another air force search plane reached the wreck of the T-6D and located the pilot's body.

The following day, San Bernardino County coroner E.P. Doyle arrived at the crash site to recover Second Lieutenant Gordon A. Zempel's remains, along with representatives of the air force accident investigation team, which wanted to determine the probable cause of the fatal crash. The evidence they found at the crash site proved to be inconclusive. The pilot had not attempted to bail out but had been thrown out of the cockpit on impact, and his parachute pack had been thrown open and partially deployed. Several different scenarios were given for the crash. The T-6D had run out of fuel in one tank, and the pilot was unable to switch to the other tank before he stalled and spun in; or after the pilot had flown into a small valley surrounded by high ridges, he had been unable to clear a ridge in his flight path when he turned too steeply, stalled his aircraft and spun in. But what actually happened will never be known, as there were no witnesses. The investigators recommended that the local flying area for reservists be modified to exclude the nearby mountains.

The Zempel family finally had closure and began preparations for the funeral of their beloved son and brother. Second Lieutenant Gordon A. Zempel, age twenty-three, who had volunteered in 1942 to help defend our nation, was buried with full military honors.

On March 24, 1954, a speedy civilian Beechcraft Staggerwing N65K, painted bright yellow, departed Burbank Airport in the metropolitan Los Angeles area with pilot John A. White and three female passengers on board. Their destination was Calexico, California. It was raining at the time of the departure, and when Mr. White radioed the Ontario Airport tower twenty minutes later, he asked for permission to land there, as the weather was deteriorating rapidly. Mr. White's last transmission was heard a few minutes later when he stated he was flying at nine thousand feet AGL in icing conditions, and he then asked for emergency landing instructions at March

NAA AT-6 Texan advanced trainer (other designations are SNJ and Harvard) similar to that flown by Second Lieutenant Gordon A. Zempel on January 24, 1948. Here, Chris LeFave prepares for takeoff from Zamperini Field with Tom Maloney in the back seat on May 18, 2013. *Photo by G.P. Macha.*

Second Lieutenant Zempel's AT-6D went missing on January 24, 1948, but it was not found until August 6. The crash site is located northwest of Fawnskin in the San Bernardino Mountains. The inverted tail assembly and empennage are clearly visible. *Photo courtesy Ben Giebler.*

AFB in Riverside County. The next day, N65K was posted as missing, and an extensive search effort was launched. The air force, civil air patrol and sheriffs' departments from four California counties were involved. A wreck was spotted thirty miles east of San Diego, California, on March 28, but it turned out to be the old wreckage of a Luscombe light aircraft that had crashed several years earlier. The weeks passed and became months and, then, years. Still no trace of N65K was seen.

The Beechcraft Staggerwing was a 1930s design that was produced until 1948 with a delivery interruption during World War II. N65K was a G-17S variant powered by one 450-horsepower Pratt & Whitney Wasp Junior nine-cylinder radial engine The Staggerwing was fast for its time, cruising at 198 miles per hour. The materials used to build the Model 17 included wood, wielded tubular metal and some aluminum skin, but the majority fuselage and wing skin covering was fabric. The Model 17 had retractable landing gear, giving the Staggerwing a pleasing appearance that made it popular among owners around the world.

With the passing of time, the fate of Mr. White and his three passengers—Joan Belger, Bobbie Gay and Floradel Kidwell—was largely forgotten until October 24, 1959, when a young civil air patrol cadet, Richard Usen, happened upon remains of N65K while hiking off the trail above the North Fork of Lytle Creek in the eastern San Gabriel Mountains of San Bernardino County. Scattered among the smashed debris of the long-missing Staggerwing were personal effects and human bones. The most important part of the mystery was solved with the wreckage being found, but how N65K ended up on the north side of the mountains below the Baldy Notch will never be known.

John A. White might have become completely lost in the blinding rain and snowstorm that dark night in March and might have been trying desperately to return to Burbank, having completed a 180-degree turn, not realizing that he was north of the San Gabriel Mountains. Hikers going off the trail would find more missing aircraft wrecks in San Bernardino County in the years to come.

George C. Bechtel was a successful businessman from Southgate, California. He owned a refrigeration company and a four-seat Piper PA-22 Tri-Pacer N7046B. The Tri-Pacer was a popular 1950s-era light aircraft that was easy to fly and maintain. It had tricycle landing gear and was a fabric-covered, high-wing light aircraft powered by a 150-horsepower Lycoming O-320 engine. Mr. Bechtel enjoyed flying with his family on short hops around Southern California in his PA-22. On October 28, 1956, he departed the Apple Valley Airport in San Bernardino County with his wife, Dorothy, and their twelve-year-old daughter, Vicki Lou, bound for Fullerton Airport in Orange County. Mr. Bechtel would normally return from flights to the Mojave Desert area via the Cajon Pass, but weather conditions that day were becoming dicey because of an approaching cold front. Clouds obscured the passes and the local mountains, winds were increasing and rain was falling in the San Bernardino Valley. When the Bechtel family did not arrive at Fullerton Airport as expected, a search was initiated on October 29. Poor weather hampered early search efforts, but when the weather improved, the civil air patrol, along with aircraft from the Los Angeles and San Bernardino County Sheriffs' Departments, flew extensive search missions for more than two weeks. The USAF search-and-rescue unit based at March AFB joined the effort, too, but without result.

In November, 7046 Baker joined the CAP list of missing and unaccounted-for aircraft in California, which, at that time, numbered more than a dozen aircraft. The civil air patrol alerted their pilots and ground search personnel to keep an eye out for the missing Tri-Pacer in the San Bernardino and San Gabriel Mountain areas. Finally, on June 6, 1960, a hiker traveling off trail near 8,900-foot Cucamonga Peak stumbled on the crumpled, unburned wreckage of the Bechtels' PA-22. Inside were the skeletal remains of the Bechtel family. The Civil Aeronautics Board report indicated that death was instantaneous for those on board, a small consolation for the next of kin. Wreckage of the PA-22 was not that hard to see once the authorities knew where to look; the white fabric with red pinstripes provided a good contrast to the pine trees that surrounded the site. In winter, however, with snow blanketing the mountains, it would have been impossible to see any of the wreckage. A pilot or pilots flying near the wreck might have seen the Tri-Pacer but dismissed it as an old wreck, one of dozens that are located in the eastern San Gabriel Mountains. When possible, crash sites are marked and painted with red or yellow Xs, indicating that they are known wrecks. Over time, the paint used to mark wrecks can fade, making it very difficult in some cases to know whether a crash site should be reported or not. When in doubt, report what you see and note the location as best as possible, GPS being the best possible technology to use in marking the accident site. N7046B was not marked but pushed over a cliff into a deep ravine, where it remains today.

In the 1950s, the general aviation revolution was in full swing as airports were packed to their limits with small private aircraft tied down outside and in hangars for those lucky enough to afford to have one. Beechcraft, Cessna and Piper were the big three in private aircraft manufacturing.

They produced fine aircraft that sold well in the United States and around the world, too. Pilots could go almost anywhere at almost any time in them—*almost* being the operative word.

On March 2, 1957, Marjorie King of Westwood near Los Angeles and her mother, Marjorie Kumler, of La Jolla, California, departed from Los Angeles International Airport with Mr. and Mrs. Jacob Wierdma of Kent, Great Britain. The Wierdmas were interested in purchasing a property in the Colorado Desert area, and Ms. King had agreed to fly them there in her white-and-yellow Cessna 170A, an all-metal, four-seat, high-wing monoplane with a cruising speed of 120 miles per hour. The Wierdmas were reported to have been carrying $5,000 in cash for a down payment if they found a suitable property. They departed Los Angeles International Airport at 11:15 a.m., but as they flew east, they encountered a fast-moving winter storm front that was arriving over the mountains of Southern California, enshrouding them and the San Gorgonio Pass in dense clouds with rain showers and snow falling at higher elevations. As the front closed in, Ms. King, a capable pilot with fifteen years of flying experience, might have been having trouble knowing exactly where she was. Flying through the San Gorgonio Pass was essential to reaching their initial destination in Palm Springs, but the pilot might not have been able to tell whether she had entered the pass or not. A life-and-death decision was now at hand: continue eastward in the poor visibility or execute a 180-degree turn and fly back to LAX.

Marjorie King's choice seems to have been to continue, but at some point on the stormy afternoon of March 2, she turned back toward the Los Angeles Basin and tragically flew into the annals of aviation accident history. As with earlier cases of missing aircraft, the search effort was extensive and lengthy. It was thought, at the time, that the Cessna 170A would be found on the north side of the San Gorgonio Pass because of reports from residents living in the Yucaipa and Oak Glen communities who stated they heard a light aircraft flying east between 1:00 and 1:30 p.m. on March 2. San Bernardino County deputy sheriff Willard Farquhar was in charge of the search effort, and he interviewed several of the witnesses who claimed they heard the sound of an aircraft engine but could not see the aircraft because of the heavy cloud cover. One promising report came from a ranch east of Oak Glen, nestled at the base of towering eight- and nine-thousand-foot peaks. It was in this rugged area that the search effort was concentrated. When the weather improved, aerial searches intensified along with those of highly skilled ground teams. The spring snow was gone by late June 1957, but still no trace of the missing Cessna was found. Finally, in the fall of 1957, the final search missions were flown, and the last volunteer ground teams ended their efforts, too.

The years passed. The winter storms came and went, and other aircraft went missing and were found, but not N1391D. In the mid-1960s, Willard Farquhar continued a one-man search in the Vivian Creek, Forest Home and Valley of the Falls regions north of Oak Glen. I hiked with him on one occasion in the summer of 1965 on my day off work from a nearby mountain summer camp at Barton Flats. Deputy Sheriff Farquhar was convinced Marjorie King had flown into Mill Creek Canyon, surrounded on three sides by peaks ranging from 7,000 feet to the 11,500-foot Mount San Gorgonio. At the east end of the 7-mile-long canyon was the precipitous Mill Creek Jumpoff. It was a perfect box from which there could be little chance of escape, especially while flying in a winter storm. Deputy Farquhar told me he hoped some of the Cessna 170A wreckage would have washed down into Mill Creek, as had the wreckage of the 1945 Vought F4U-1D Corsair. He was also focused on the Vivian Creek area that drained into Mill Creek from the northeast side of the canyon. We found no trace of aircraft wreckage on that hot summer day, but Deputy Farquhar was undaunted. His personal search continued until October 18, 1973, when the search for another missing light aircraft resolved the Marjorie King case.

A civil air patrol pilot spotted the wreckage of an aircraft that he could not identify, and that led the San Bernardino County Sheriffs' Aviation Unit to launch a helicopter and ground search team. The ground team arrived at the wreckage of a Mooney Mk 20E N1385W that had crashed on May 7, 1971, killing a young married couple and its baby, but this was a known wreckage, not the one the CAP pilot had seen. The sheriffs' helicopter pilot and his observer spotted the unknown wreck about one thousand feet from the Mooney Mk20E, and the ground team was then directed to that location, where they reported finding a white-and-yellow single-engine civilian lightplane with the registration number of N1391D. Now, Inspector Willard Farquhar was ecstatic; the long sixteen-year search had ended and closure for the next of kin achieved.

In the 1970s, I set out to discover why the Cessna 170A ended up on the east flank of the San Bernardino Mountains, nowhere near the primary search area, and why almost no human remains were present at the crash site, not to mention what happened to the alleged $5,000 reported to be on board.

Marjorie King apparently made it through the San Gorgonio Pass, or perhaps over the San Bernardino Mountains themselves, and then executed a 180-degree turn in an effort to reach the San Bernardino Valley, or possibly

LAX beyond. Inspector Farquhar told me in an interview dated August 27, 1976, that he checked the records at the sheriffs' substation closest to the crash site in Yucca Valley and that an elderly resident of Pioneer Town had reported seeing a small fire burning high on the mountain west of his home on the late afternoon of March 2. Understandably, perhaps no connection was made between the fire and the missing Cessna at that time. Nor was the report of a fire taken seriously, since heavy snow covered that mountain. Nonetheless, Inspector Farquhar told me that he believed the report was directly related to the crash of Marjorie King's Cessna 170A since there was evidence of a post-impact fire at the accident scene that probably consumed any cash on board.

The absence of radio messages, appeals for assistance or Mayday calls were probably because Marjorie King was too busy flying her airplane, totally focused on getting out of the clouds and to the safe haven of an airport. The lack of human remains was explained by Inspector Farquhar, who stated in an interview with the *San Bernardino Sun* newspaper that "black bear are common in the crash area, and that they may have taken the remains." If not bear, then coyotes or pack rats certainly would have helped themselves, too. The wreckage of Cessna 170A N1391D still lies unmarked on a steep slope of the San Bernardino Mountains in a rugged area where the Project Remembrance Team located it on August 14, 2013.

The rugged mountains of San Bernardino County can conceal the wrecks of missing aircraft, and so can the open and expansive vastness of the Mojave Desert. Flying long distances in a small aircraft can be problematic at any time of year. Many factors, including pilot skill, aircraft maintenance, flight planning, weather and time of day, can contribute to an accident scenario.

Labor Day weekend 1962 at Big Bear Lake was clear and warm, a perfect destination for a pilot to fly his wife and two young daughters to visit family and friends. The pilot's father-in-law had a fine home in the town of Big Bear Lake where everyone could stay, relax, visit and enjoy this beautiful part of the San Bernardino Mountains. After a two-night stay, it was time for the young family to return to their home in San Diego. They departed from Big Bear City Airport on the afternoon of September 3 with the proviso that the pilot would phone his father-in-law upon their safe arrival back at Montgomery Field. When the confirmation call was not made, the pilot's father-in-law notified the SBCSD that Piper PA-28 Cherokee N9358W was missing with four loved ones on board. Search missions were launched the following day, and ground search teams were mobilized also. The high peaks of the San Gorgonio wilderness were scoured, including San Bernardino,

Pat J. Macha at the crash site of Mooney MK 20E N1385W, in which a family of three perished on May 7, 1971. The wreckage is marked with red and orange *X*s to prevent hikers and fliers from thinking it is a missing aircraft. *Photo by Fred Moore.*

The smashed remains of Cessna 170 N1391D that had four persons on board when it vanished on March 2, 1957. The wreck was accidentally discovered on October 18, 1973, during the search for another missing aircraft. *Photo courtesy Inspector Willard Farquhar.*

109

East San Bernardino, Anderson and Sheilds. Keller Peak, a known plane catcher, was carefully scrutinized, as was a host of peaks and mountains in San Diego County. September 4 and 5 passed without result, but September 6 proved to be the case breaker. If the Cherokee had gone down shortly after takeoff, the plane and its occupants could be nearby. The grandfather's gut feeling was his beloved family were close by, and while riding in a helicopter, he spotted his son's white with green striped PA-28. The helicopter pilot radioed ground teams to immediately proceed to the crash site, located less than a mile from the grandfather's home.

Stan Jones of San Diego, a close family friend, participated in the search, and he was one of the first to reach the wreck of Piper PA-28 N9358W. What follows is from a letter received from Mr. Jones in December 1999:

Sitting with the two girls for over half an hour before others arrived and surveying the scene, it was plain to see that the pilot had guided the descending aircraft directly into a grove of young saplings which would have cushioned the impact considerably and altered the outcome. Tragically, a snag[ged] conifer caught the plane's left wing, shearing it off at the root and opening the fuselage panels. This terrific force abruptly changed the direction of the Cherokee from due south to due east and smack into a ninety-foot massive [ponderosa pine] five feet in circumference.

The resulting impact snapped the prop shaft, leaving the propeller imbedded in the thick bark some [fifty to sixty feet] above the ground. One of the girls murmured, "Daddy said we're not going to make [it] over the trees."

The only cabin door was blocked, but the pilot exited on his side through the shattered and loose aluminum panels, lifting each daughter out and to the ground. The pilot then told his daughters, "We'll be found; don't be afraid, mommy's asleep." He propped himself against the trunk of a fallen tree, and the girls huddled at his feet. One of them had retrieved vitamin pills and made three nests in the pine needles. "Breakfast, lunch, dinner," they said. When the rescue crews arrived, they put the girls in rescue baskets and carried them to where a helicopter could land. They were rushed to St. Bernadine's Hospital in San Bernardino.

The eldest girl was eight and in critical condition. Her younger sister was six but not seriously injured. They had survived three days and nights without food or water. The nights were cold, and though badly injured, the eldest sister crawled back into the plane and found a suitcase with their

Piper PA-28 Cherokee N9358W with members of the San Bernardino Sheriffs' Department examining the accident scene. Two parents died, and two young daughters survived on September 3, 1962. *Photo courtesy Fred Beam.*

father's clothes inside. The girls put on the clothes to keep warm. On the third day, both girls saw several search planes fly by, and then, a helicopter appeared, though the girls had no way of knowing that their grandfather was on board. They were saved, surviving a tragedy that claimed both of their parents; they would be loved and cared for by the very grandparents they had come to visit in Big Bear City.

I visited the Piper PA-28 crash site in the summer of 1967. The forest was dark, shadowed and damp after the passage of a thunderstorm. Little remained of the aircraft, but an intact engine cowling was still there, along with numerous small parts and broken pieces of Plexiglas. Any visitor could see why the once-missing plane had been so hard to find in this dense and overgrown place. I interviewed Civil Aeronautics Board investigator Fred Beam a few years later about the accident. He told me that when the pilot realized he was going to crash, he turned the electrical switch off, thereby reducing the risk of a post-impact fire. He also said "tears of joy were shed" when he went to the PA-28 site because the little girls had somehow managed to survive it all.

The disappearance of a Bellanca Model 14-19 N9816B, a four-seat light aircraft, on February 6, 1976, would follow a familiar pattern of a flight plan being filed as VFR when the weather report indicated that IFR conditions might be encountered along the projected flight path. The Bellanca departed Santa Barbara, California, with a pilot and three passengers on board. They were headed to Mexico on a volunteer medical assistance mission. Rain and snow showers had obscured the San Gabriel and San Bernardino Mountains on February 6 and for several days thereafter, hampering search efforts. The civil air patrol flew extensive search missions over a wide area without result, and the winter snowfall made matters worse, blanketing the Southern California mountains in deep snow. On July 28, 1977, the mangled wreckage of the Bellanca Cruisemaster was spotted at 9,500 feet MSL between 10,691-foot East San Bernardino Peak and 10,864-foot Anderson Peak, well off the intended flight path to Mexicali, Mexico. The recovery of the bodies was very difficult because of the nearly vertical terrain at the crash site. The wreckage of N9816B was not salvaged or marked with red *X*s because it was just too dangerous to attempt.

Sixty-year-old Bob Wakeman was a proud owner of a Mooney Mk20K N3624H. On August 5, 1983, Mr. Wakeman planned to fly from Tulsa, Oklahoma, with his son-in-law Jim Huffman and Huffman's five-year-old son, Grant, to Fullerton, California, via the Grand Canyon in Arizona. A summer flight across desert lands can include dodging thunderstorms and the ups and downs associated with clear air turbulence generated from heat rising off the desert.

Flying on a moonless, cloudless night across the desert can present problems during a VFR flight when there are few illuminated ground references visible, which can possibly lead to pilot disorientation. Using the autopilot can help, but in moderate-to-severe turbulence, the autopilot can be overwhelmed, leading to loss of aircraft control.

Mr. Wakeman reached the Grand Canyon for a dinner and refueling stop about 6:00 p.m. on August 5. He then continued on toward his destination in Fullerton with good weather forecast for the flight across the Mojave Desert. When he failed to arrive at Fullerton Airport, a search effort was launched. While the weather had been favorable on August 5, severe turbulence hampered search efforts a week later. Meanwhile, the anguish and uncertainty felt by family members and friends of the missing intensified. The heartbreaking elements in all stories of the missing must never be downplayed or trivialized.

Following weeks of ground and air searching without results, efforts were scaled back. The mountains of the Eastern Mojave Desert had been scoured, as had the eastern flanks of the San Bernardino and San Jacinto Mountains and the San Gorgonio Pass. The Santa Ana Mountains and the Chino Hills near Fullerton Airport were thoroughly searched. Mrs. Carol Wakeman was quoted as saying that "not knowing the fate of her husband and the others on board had given her empathy for the families of MIAs, hostages, and the families of the missing Cessna 336." It was because of a search for another missing plane that her husband's Mooney MK20K was finally found on January 21, 1991, after eight long years, thanks to a sharp-eyed volunteer observer whose own daughter was missing aboard the Cessna 336 N3848U.

The San Bernardino County Sheriffs' Department confirmed that the site was in fact the missing Mooney Mk20K, N3624H on January 22, and the County Coroner's Office recovered the remains within a few days. The National Transportation Safety Board sent investigator George Petterson to the crash site in an effort to determine the cause of the accident. After a lengthy investigation, the NTSB issued the following statement: "An in-flight loss of control for undetermined reasons." N3624H was equipped with an emergency locator transmitter (ELT), but it failed to function properly due to the nature of the high-speed impact on the desert. The ELT has been mandated by the FAA for all general aviation and commercial aircraft since 1973, and it has helped save many lives and helped bring many searches to a speedy conclusion. The ELT cannot survive 100 percent of all accidents in working order, especially if there is transmitter-antenna separation, post-impact fire, impact damage to the unit itself or poor maintenance of the ELT and its battery.

One missing aircraft had been found, but a Cessna 336 Skymaster, N3848U, was still unaccounted for. This five-seat, twin-engine, twin-boom lightplane had departed Bullhead City, Arizona, on November 14, 1991, bound for Fullerton, California, with five persons on board. The pilot obtained a weather briefing from the FAA Flight Service Station that forecast obscurations (clouds) around the mountains and passes along the flight route. He had made this flight many times before and probably thought he could do it again, so he did not file a flight plan. The civil air patrol search coordinators knew that the Cessna 336 would probably be found in the approaches to the San Gorgonio Pass or, perhaps, near the Cajon Pass, called by some a "backdoor" entry into the Greater Los Angeles Basin.

Another factor in the disappearance was the late departure from Bullhead City Airport, sometime around 3:00 p.m. By the time the Cessna

The tail of Mooney MK 20K N3624H that was carrying three family members when it vanished on August 5, 1983. On January 21, 1991, the wreckage was finally spotted only a few miles north of Interstate 40 during a search for another missing aircraft. *Photo courtesy George Petterson.*

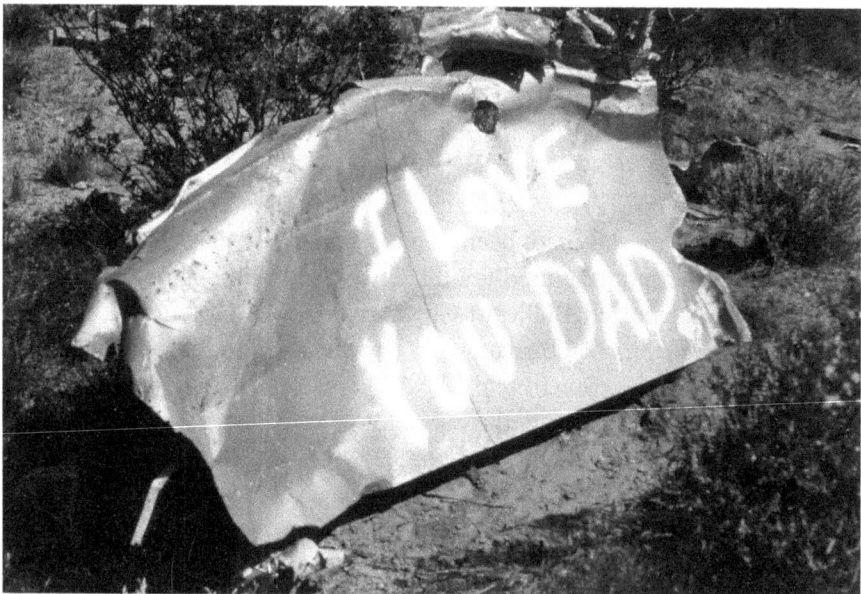

The wreckage of N3624H became a memorial when a grieving family member visited the crash site to leave a heartfelt message. *Photo courtesy George Petterson.*

was approaching the mountain passes, it was almost twilight, when the combination of clouds, haze and the setting sun would make it difficult for the pilot to see where he was going. A marginal VFR flight was rapidly becoming an IFR situation.

The search effort for the missing Skymaster would involve hundreds of pilots and observers from the civil air patrol, plus additional personnel from the Riverside and San Bernardino Counties Sheriffs' Aviation Units. Nearly twenty-five thousand square miles of desert and mountains would be searched for three weeks before the search would be called off on December 5, 1991, due in part to heavy snowfall in the mountains of Southern California. The CAP promised to renew the search if new evidence or leads were found.

Intermittent search sorties were made by volunteers during the spring months of 1992 without result until members of the missing pilot's family decided to conduct their own search effort that summer after the snows had largely melted. The father of the missing pilot would not give up, and at great expense, he chartered a helicopter and began searching the San Bernardino Mountains north and northwest of Big Bear Lake along a route he suspected his son might have taken seven months earlier. On the last day of the helicopter search, fortune smiled, albeit sadly, as a devoted father spotted the crash site of his beloved son. The smashed and unburned wreckage of the Cessna 336 Skymaster was found on a rugged pine-covered mountain, thirteen air miles from Big Bear Lake. At last, the remains of the missing would be recovered and laid to rest. The grieving next of kin and their friends could have closure, rest and, hopefully, peace of mind.

Most aircraft that are posted missing do so during periods of severe weather, heavy rain, snow and high winds, but not always, as was the case of a USMC Rockwell International OV-10A Bronco Bu No 155485 with a crew of two on board. The pilot was Captain Sergio R. Vivaldi, USMCR, assigned to Marine Observation Squadron 2 (VMO-2). In the back seat was First Lieutenant Joel H. Piehl, also assigned to VMO-2 at USMC Camp Pendleton in San Diego County, California. Captain Vivaldi did not file a flight plan on the morning of August 24, 1989, and he did not request a formal weather briefing. But the weather was good across all Southern California. Cumulus clouds were scattered across the region, and there were no alto cumulus buildups associated with summer thunderstorms. Visibility was generally characterized as unlimited, and only light turbulence was reported in the desert areas. When OV-10A Bu No 155485 call sign "Hostage 55" and its crew failed to return to the airfield at Camp Pendleton, they were posted as missing. Search missions were authorized to commence the following day, August 25, 1989.

Cessna 336 Skymaster N3848U went missing with five family members on board on November 14, 1991. It was located on July 5, 1992, thanks to helicopter search flights paid for by the father of the missing pilot. *Photo courtesy John Zimmerman.*

Since no flight plan had been filed, the civil air patrol had little idea of where to begin looking for Hostage 55. The OV-10A has a unique appearance, characterized by twin turbo prop engines on a twin boom layout with the horizontal stabilizer mounted high on the tail. The wings are stubby, and the two-man crew sits one behind the other forward of the wings in a high-visibility cockpit equipped with ejection seats. The OV-10A Bronco began service with the USMC in 1968, and it was phased out of USMC service in the OV-10D version in 1995. The mission of the Bronco was that of a light attack and forward air control aircraft capable of operating from dirt airstrips, roadways or other unimproved surfaces. The Bronco was highly maneuverable and a pleasure to fly, and it remains in military service with several foreign air forces today.

The marine corps, civil air patrol and other agencies involved in the search effort hoped that there would be public input that would provide leads in this difficult case. There were two reports of interest that did come in: a column of black smoke was seen on the eastern flank of the San Gorgonio wilderness area above the Middle Fork of the Whitewater River, and a woman hiking near the North Fork of the Whitewater River said she had heard a rumble around noon on the twenty-fourth. A U.S. Forest Service helicopter was dispatched where the smoke had been reported, but nothing unusual was seen. At this point, one civil air patrol pilot, Lieutenant Colonel Keith Kelly of Squadron 195, was determined to search the Whitewater Canyon area, especially since there was a report of an OV-10A having been seen flying in the Banning Pass near the noon hour on the day the Bronco vanished. Kelly planned to fly his Cessna 177 Cardinal, call sign "Rescue 47" with two trained observers—Captain Al Seidler of CAP Squadron 35, sitting behind him, and Lieutenant Colonel Banner Rice of CAP Squadron 195, sitting in the right front seat. The trio flew to the place where the smoke had been seen and found two old plane wrecks and areas burned by lightning strikes but no sign of what they hoped to find, the missing USMC observation plane. Their next sortie was on September 7, and they returned to the same general area to continue the search effort. This time, they spotted something orange in color, but turbulent air with powerful updrafts and downdrafts made it unsafe to linger. The next day, they flew back to the canyon, arriving there at 6:45 a.m., and spent one hour searching until a San Bernardino County Sheriffs' helicopter pilot arrived, asking if he could help out.

Kelly directed the helicopter to the area where they had seen something orange the preceding day, and the helicopter pilot reported that his observer had seen something, too. A moment later, the pilot said, "We've got your wreckage!" It was Lieutenant Colonel Keith P. Kelley's seventieth birthday. What a relief, success and closure for the next of kin and friends of the missing marine officers, who been found thanks to a skilled CAP pilot and his observer crew who would not give up the search. Kelly flew south to Palm Springs Airport, where a USMC CH-46 Seaknight helicopter was waiting to launch to confirm the crash site of the OV-10A. Once that sad mission was accomplished, the marines signaled, "No further assistance needed, sir."

Lieutenant Colonel Kelly had "reasoned" that the OV-10A had followed the Whitewater River into the rising terrain of the San Bernardino Mountains, and at a critical junction, Captain Sergio R. Vivaldi had chosen to continue flying up the Middle Fork of the Whitewater. As soon as he made that turn into the canyon, "he had been trapped like a fly in a spider's web." Unable to fly out of the trap, he faced the "terrifying" cliff, part of a great headwall known as the Middle Fork Jumpoff. The official U.S. Marine Corps Mishap Report stated that Captain Vivaldi and First Lieutenant Piehl had successfully ejected from their aircraft but that both men had tragically fallen back onto the burning wreckage of their OV-10A. Nothing is visible at the crash site of the OV-10A today because of winter avalanches, rock falls and landslides. The Bronco and its crew went down in one of the most forbidding and remote places in the San Gorgonio wilderness.

Monetary rewards are sometimes offered in an effort to quickly resolve missing aircraft cases. One of the largest ever posted was a $50,000 reward good for one year from the date of posting for information leading to the location of Daniel Katz and his Piper PA-28-181 N8253W, missing since June 3, 2001. Mr. Katz had rented N8253W, a Piper Archer four-seat lightplane, for a flight from Brackett Field in Los Angeles County to Perris Valley Airport in Riverside County. He told the dispatcher before departing Brackett Field about 3:30 p.m. that he intended to skydive at Perris Valley and that if he had any trouble returning to Brackett, he would land at Cable Airport in Upland. Witnesses at Perris Valley stated that Mr. Katz departed from there at 7:15 p.m. The return flight from Perris Valley should have been uneventful, except that low stratus clouds and haze covered the Los Angeles Basin and the adjoining valleys. This weather pattern of night and morning low clouds is common in coastal Southern California during the months of May and June. "June Gloom" is a common acronym used to describe the dense clouds that bring light rain or drizzle along the foothills of the San Gabriel and San Bernardino Mountains. This weather pattern is also common in September and October and is not usually associated with storm fronts. Sometimes pilots underestimate the dangers of VFR flight in these conditions, making the aforementioned months some of the most dangerous, resulting in higher accident rates for aircraft losses in southwestern San Bernardino County.

Mr. Katz contacted March Air Force Base air traffic control and asked for flight following and said that he would proceed VFR to Brackett Field. The radar track showed that N8253W was heading north over San Bernardino and starting to turn left. Mr. Katz then radioed that he was seventeen to eighteen miles from Brackett at about 7:30 p.m. Less than two minutes later, radar contact was lost at the mouth of the Lytle Creek Canyon. Going off the radar was not unusual for a small aircraft flying near the mountains, and since no formal flight plan had been filed, it was not until June 6, 2001, that the aircraft rental operator notified authorities that Daniel Katz was overdue and presumed missing. The civil air patrol launched an extensive search effort focused on the last known radar plot of N8253W. The speculation was intense about where the Piper Archer might have crashed—Cajon Pass; the South, Middle and North Forks of the Lytle Creek; the south-facing foothills of the San Gabriel Mountains all the way into Los Angeles County. It was thought that Mr. Katz had possibly overshot Brackett Field in the clouds and darkness, possibly crashing in the Angeles National Forest. There was no ELT signal received from the downed Piper, no eyewitnesses, no wreckage and no motive to purposefully disappear. The Katz family understandably wanted to know the where, how and why of their son's loss. To this end, the cash reward was offered to hopefully bring the search effort to a successful conclusion. It also helped to guarantee that when formal search missions ceased, private individuals and volunteer organizations would be motivated to continue the hunt.

After one year, the $50,000 reward offer expired with no result, and it was then reduced to $10,000 in the hope that some interested parties might continue to look for the beloved member of the Katz family. But as the years passed, interest faded in what was becoming a very cold case. On August 15, 2007, I gave a presentation to the San Bernardino County Sheriffs' Aviation Unit about aircraft accident sites within their county. I was asked at that time where I thought Daniel Katz and his Piper Archer could be found. My answer was the same as that given to the CAP in 2001. I said, "In my opinion, you will find him in the South Fork, Middle Fork or North Fork of the Lytle Creek"—an area in which a number of other long-missing aircraft have been found.

On September 28, 2008, I received an e-mail from the SBSD Aviation Unit that one of their helicopters, crewed by Deputies Shawn Moore and Jeff Karp, was conducting a routine patrol of the Lytle Creek area when they spotted what they believed to be the wreckage of Piper Archer N8253W in the Middle Fork of the Lytle Creek. Not everyone had forgotten after all.

A few days later, I was invited to view the accident site from the air and witness the recovery of N8253W by a team of specialists who had to be airlifted to a ridge above the crash site. They were assigned the task of cutting the wreckage into three sections to facilitate the recovery. One wing had be separated from the fuselage on impact, but otherwise, the Piper Archer was unburned and remarkably intact, albeit on a forbiddingly steep canyon wall.

As we approached the accident scene in a Hughes 500D helicopter, the pilot asked, "Can you see the Piper?" I said, "No, I don't." As the 500D was hovering, the pilot said, "I'm going to point now," and thanks to him, I could then clearly see the wreck and understand why it had not been found by aerial searchers. The paint scheme on the Archer was tan, and although there were brown and gold pinstripe accents, the wreckage blended into the background. Being on the north side of the precipitous ridgeline, the wreckage was often in the shadows and, in the winter season, covered by snow. There is a road in the canyon bottom that was used in the recovery

Crash site of Piper PA-28-181 Archer N8253W on mountain ridge in the Middle Fork of Lytle Creek as seen from a helicopter on October 3, 2008, during wreckage-recovery operations. *Photo by G.P. Macha.*

View of the fuselage and one wing of N8253W prior to recovery operations. *Photo by Ryan Gilmore.*

The tail assembly of N8253W being airlifted to the recovery area. *Photo by G.P. Macha.*

effort, and as NTSB investigator George Petterson noted, the wreck could be seen from where we parked with field glasses.

The entire recovery process was completed within a few hours, with the Hughes 500D flying five recovery sorties: one for each wing; one for the empennage and tail section; one for the fuselage, which included the cockpit; and the last to recover the Textron Lycoming 180-horsepower engine. The fuselage was remarkably intact, leading to speculation that the pilot might have survived the crash, albeit badly injured. It was noted that Mr. Katz had not used his shoulder harness, as it was in the stowed position. His seatbelt was also unfastened, and he might have released it himself had he survived. But we will never know the answer to that sad question. What could be answered immediately was why the emergency locator transmitter had not functioned properly, given the exterior antenna was still attached to the empennage and the ELT itself intact and securely mounted in the tail section. George Petterson's first comment was, "I want to see the switch and what position it's in." The shocking answer was that it was switched off.

When Daniel Katz rented N8253W, it was not part of his preflight protocols to crawl into the tail to check the ELT. According to Federal Aviation Administration regulations, the ELT was supposed to be in the ready position at all times. Had Daniel Katz survived the crash and the ELT worked properly, his life might have been saved. In any case, the ELT signal would have spared the Katz family the agony of not knowing the fate of their beloved son for more than seven years. Anyone who saw the Katz crash site would appreciate the ruggedness of the terrain and the inescapable box canyon into which he had accidentally flown on that cloudy, hazy evening in June 2001. It would also be clear that Mr. Katz had tried his best to extricate himself from the Middle Fork of the Lytle Creek by flying up a nearly vertical canyon wall and that he had come close to succeeding.

The emergency locator transmitter has contributed to saving the lives of more than a dozen pilots and their passengers who have crashed in San Bernardino County since 1973. The ELT has shortened many searches where there were no survivors and saved tens of thousands of dollars in the costs of both ground and aerial search efforts.

The civilian and military aircraft accident rates of the mid- to late twentieth century will not be seen again in the twenty-first because education, innovation and technological applications have made flying safer than could ever have been imagined just twenty years ago.

GLOSSARY OF TERMS

AAB: Army Air Base
AAF: Army Air Field
ADC: Air Defense Command
AFB: Air Force Base
AGL: Above Ground Level
ANG: Air National Guard
ATC: Air Traffic Control
BLM: Bureau of Land Management
CAB: Civil Aeronautics Board
CAP: Civil Air Patrol
ELT: Emergency Locator Transmitter
FAA: Federal Aviation Administration
IFR: Instrument Flight Rules
ILS: Instrument Landing System
NAA: North American Aviation
NAS: Naval Air Station
MATS: Material Air Transport Command
MCAS: Marine Corps Air Station
MSL: Mean Sea Level
NACA: National Advisory Committee for Aeronautics
NASA: National Aeronautics and Space Administration
NTSB: National Transportation Safety Board
RAPCON: Radar Approach Control
SAR: Search and Rescue

SBCSD: San Bernardino County Sheriffs' Department
TAC: Tactical Air Command
USAA: United States Army Aviation
USAAC: United States Army Corps
USAAF: United States Army Air Force
USAF: United States Air Force
USAFR: United States Air Force Reserve
USFS: United States Forest Service
USMC: United States Marine Corps
USMCR: United States Marine Corps Reserve
USN: United States Navy
USNR: United States Navy Reserve
VFR: Visual Flight Rules
VOR: Very High Frequency Omni-directional Range
WASP: Women Airforce Service Pilot

Abbreviated military aircraft designations:
A (attack)
B (bomber)
C (cargo)
F (fighter)
G (glider)
H (helicopter)
J (test)
L (liaison)
O (observation)
P (pursuit)
Q (drone)
R (reconnaissance)
T (trainer)
X (experimental)

BIBLIOGRAPHY

Books

Allen, Richard Sanders. *Revolution in the Sky: Those Fabulous Lockheeds, the Pilots Who Flew Them.* Brattleboro, VT: Stephen Greene Press, 1964.

Ellis, Glenn. *Air Crash Investigation of General Aviation Aircraft.* Greybull, WY: Capstan Publications Inc., 1984.

Françillon, René J. *Lockheed Aircraft Since 1913.* London, UK: Putnam & Company Ltd., 1982.

———. *McDonnell Douglas Aircraft Since 1920.* London, UK: Putnam & Company Ltd., 1979.

Green, William, and Gerald Pollinger. *The Aircraft of the World.* London, UK: Macdonald & Co. Ltd., 1965.

Leadabrand, Russ. *A Guidebook to the San Bernardino Mountains of California, Including Lake Arrowhead and Big Bear.* Menlo Park, CA: Lane Book Company, 1964.

Macha, Gary Patric. *Aircraft Wrecks in the Mountains and Deserts of California 1908–1990.* Huntington Beach, CA: Aircraft Archaeological Press, 1991.

———. *Aircraft Wrecks in the Mountains and Deserts of California 1909–1996.* San Clemente, CA: INFO NET Publishing, 1997.

Macha, G.P., and Don Jordan. *Aircraft Wrecks in the Mountains and Deserts of California 1909–2002.* Lake Forest, CA: INFO NET Publishing, 2002.

Mann, Bill. *Guide to 50 Interesting and Mysterious Sites in the Mojave.* Vol. 2. Barstow, CA: Shortfuse Publishing Co., 1999.

Merlin, Peter W., and Tony Moore. *X-Plane Crashes.* North Branch, MN: Specialty Press, 2008.

Miller, Jay. *The X-Planes: X-1 to X-45.* 3rd edition. Hinkley, UK: Midland Publishing, 2001.

Mireles, Anthony J. *August 1944–December 1945, Appendices, Indexes.* Vol. 3 of *Fatal Army Air Forces Aviation Accidents in the United States, 1941–1945.* Jefferson, NC: McFarland & Company Inc., 2006.

———. *Introduction: January 1941–June 1943.* Vol. 1 of *Fatal Army Air Forces Aviation Accidents in the United States, 1941–1945.* Jefferson, NC: McFarland & Company Inc., 2006

———. *July 1943–July 1944.* Vol. 2 of *Fatal Army Air Forces Aviation Accidents in the United States, 1941–1945.* Jefferson, NC: McFarland & Company Inc., 2006.

Robinson, John W. with David Money Harris. *San Bernardino Mountain Trails: 100 Hikes in Southern California.* 5th edition. Berkeley, CA: Wilderness Press, 2003.

Simpson, Jack "Suitcase." *Socrates and Suits Book II: Dialogue Between a Philosopher and a Fighter Pilot.* Philadelphia, PA: Xlibris Corporation, 2001.

Swanborough, Gordon, and Peter M. Bowers. *United States Military Aircraft Since 1909.* London, UK: Putnam Aeronautical Books; Washington, D.C.: Smithsonian Institution Press, 1989.

———. *United States Navy Aircraft Since 1911.* Washington, D.C.: Smithsonian Institution Press, 1989. Reprint. London, UK: Putnam Aeronautical Books, 1990.

Taylor, John W.R., and Gordon Swanborough. *Civil Aircraft of the World.* New York: Charles Scribner's Sons; London, UK: Ian Allen Ltd, 1974.

Veronico, Nicholas A., Ed Davis, Donald B. McComb Jr., and Michael B. McComb. *Wreckchasing 2: Commercial Aircraft.* Castro Valley, CA: Pacific Aero Press, 1996.

INTERVIEWS

Beam, Fred. Interviews by the author. 1968–69.

Farquhar, Willard. Interview by the author. 1966, 1973 and August 27, 1976.

Gates, Elgin F. Interviews by the author. 1995–2009.

Hoy, Donald J. Interview by the author. 2013.

Petterson, George. Interviews by the author. 1999–2013.

NEWSPAPERS

Los Angeles Times
Riverside Press Enterprise
San Bernardino Sun (High Desert)
San Bernardino Sun (Valley)

ACCIDENT REPORTS

Civil Aeronautics Board
Civilian Accident Reports
National Transportation Safety Board

MILITARY ACCIDENT REPORTS

Kirtland AFB. New Mexico HQAFSCJA.
Maxwell AFB. Alabama AFHRA/RSA.
Naval History & Heritage Command. Washington, D.C.
Naval Safety Center. Norfolk, VA.
Western Museum of Flight. Zamperini Field. Torrance, CA.

VIDEO

Macha, G. Pat. *Wreck Finding: "Lost But Not Forgotten."* DVD. Wreck Finder Productions, 1995.

WEBSITES

AAIR-Aviation Archaeological Investigation & Research. Craig Fuller. http://www.aviationarchaeology.com.
Abandoned & Little-Known Airfields. Paul Freeman. http://www.airfields-freeman.com.
Aircraft Wrecks in the Mountains and Deserts of the American West. G.P. Macha. www.aircraftwrecks.com.

LETTERS

Gates, Elgin F. to G.P. Macha. Dozens received over a thirteen-year period. 1996–2009.
Jones, Stan to G.P. Macha. One letter only. December 2, 1999.
Koch, Robert to G.P. Macha. Several dozen received. 1982–1991.

ABOUT THE AUTHOR

G. Pat Macha was born in Santa Monica, California. He is a graduate of Long Beach State College with a BA in history and a minor in geography, and he received his master's degree from Azuza Pacific University. He taught at Hawthorne High School for thirty-five years and is married and the father of two, with five grandchildren. He has authored three books on aircraft accidents in California and is a well-received speaker on aviation safety and accident histories. Pat has been documenting crash sites throughout California in remote locations for fifty years. Since 1996, along with the Project Remembrance Team, he has assisted next of kin in visiting crash sites. To learn more about his work, visit www.aircraftwrecks.com.

www.ingramcontent.com/pod-product-compliance
Lightning Source LLC
Chambersburg PA
CBHW060809100426
42813CB00004B/1010